BRAND IMAGE AND BRAND MANAGEMENT IN THE DIGITAL WORLD

AHMET CIMER

"Brands exist not to leave a mark on the world, but to make a place in people's hearts!"

ISTANBUL, 2025

AUTHOR BIOGRAPHY

Ahmet Çimer is a real-world professional, entrepreneur, senior executive researcher, strategist, and expert who has long observed how brands evolve, disintegrate, and rebuild in the digital age. His work focuses on consumer psychology, perception management, and the socio-cultural consequences of digital transformation, treating brand management as a living system rather than a static commercial structure.

With over 35 years of experience in both management and operations, Ahmet Çimer has witnessed the growth of numerous companies, from the earliest stages of brand formation to their emergence as trusted market players. This long-term perspective supports his belief that brands derive their true power not solely through visibility but through meaning, trust, and emotional resonance.

In this book, he combines contemporary brand theory with real-world observations, offering a forward-looking framework that places human connection at the heart of digital innovation. Based in Istanbul, Çimer continues to research how brands can articulate their purpose, enhance their credibility, and create sustainable value in an increasingly complex technological environment.

Born in Istanbul in 1973, Ahmet Çimer is married to Nursel Çimer and is the father of two children, Kerem Ziya and Muhammed Furkan.

To my family and all my loved ones, with my respect..

PREFACE

This book treats the brand not merely as a name, symbol, or design, but as an integrated system of meaning, perception, and interaction. The multi-layered interplay among brand image, consumer perception, and purchasing behavior is being redefined in today's digitized marketing ecosystem and is gaining an ever-deeper conceptual dimension.

In this context, the opening chapters present the theoretical foundations of brand image, perception management, and consumer behavior; the psychological and behavioral components of brand value are explained through the models of pioneering researchers such as Aaker, Keller, Kapferer, and Hollebeek. Subsequent chapters integrate this theoretical framework with the dynamics of today's digital transformation. For digitalization has radically transformed not only brands' visibility strategies but also their communication methods, trust-building techniques, personality structures, and even cultural roles.

The second part of the book examines how brand strategies are being reshaped in the digital world. Here, the differences between pre- and post-digital brand-management paradigms are systematically evaluated, and the impact of the shift from one-way communication to interactive, data-driven structures on the branding process is analyzed. Brand image is no longer merely a 'product of perception' but a dynamic organism that lives in the digital realm, continuously evolving through user interactions. This shift demonstrates that brands are now responsible not just for producing messages but for generating meaning.

The third chapter holistically addresses the core concepts of digital brand management—data-driven strategies, omnichannel experience, digital brand personality, content marketing, user-generated content (UGC), and trust-based brand building. This section reveals that brands have evolved into digital organisms that no longer merely offer products but create meaning, community, and trust. Data analytics, personalized experiences, content marketing, and social media interactions now represent a brand's emotional intelligence. Thus, branding in the digital age is not just a technical process but an emotional, cultural, and ethical journey.

Our connection with brands is no longer limited to the products we purchase. Sometimes, our reason for choosing a brand may stem from the emotions it evokes, its values, or the stance it represents. Even a subtle change in a brand's style can directly influence a consumer's lifestyle and identity. This is why how a brand is perceived forms the foundation of its relationship with consumers. It's not just about product-brand alignment; the emotional fit between brand and consumer is the strongest determinant of a brand's market success.

In my book, I examine how brand perception affects consumer behavior from both traditional marketing theories and the perspective of digital transformation. Using examples from global brands such as Apple, McDonald's, Nike, Tesla, Starbucks, and Patagonia, I analyze how a brand's symbolic meaning contributes to the construction of identity and values. Studies conducted in the food, fashion, technology, and service sectors show that, despite sectoral differences, brand image is shaped by similar psychological mechanisms: trust, perceived quality, associations, and loyalty.

Sometimes we encounter the pursuit of innovation in an Apple store, the comfort of habit in a McDonald's menu, or the power of inspiration in a Nike ad. In these moments, the same questions arise in our minds: "What are these brands really telling us?" and "As consumers, do we truly understand what brands want to convey?" These questions define both the starting point and the goal of this work: to reinterpret the interplay between brand image, perception management, and consumer behavior within the evolving realities of the digital age.

Throughout my research, I listened not only to academic sources but also to industry practices, the strategic intentions of brand creators, and—most importantly—to consumer experiences. While exploring the world of brands, I analyzed their value propositions, emotional codes, and digital behaviors. I sincerely thank all the brand stories, industry case studies, and academic works that inspired me during this process.

I hope this work will contribute not only to academic literature but also serve as a guiding resource for professionals who shape branding processes, entrepreneurs aiming to create new brands, and young researchers continuing to learn in this field. Today, brands need to be not just visible but felt—because in the digital age, success arises not from mere awareness but from trust, meaning, and continuity.

Istanbul – 2025 Ahmet Çimer

ABBREVIATIONS

CBBE	Customer-Based Brand Equity
CBE	Customer Brand Engagement
H & M	Hennes & Mauritz
AMA	American Marketing Association
UGC	User Generated Contect

LIST OF TABLES

Table 1. "The Specific effects of brand image on consumer behaviour." (Page 41)

Table 2. "The Elements of Digital Brand Management" (Page 66)

Table 3. "Comparison of brand approaches before and after digitalization" (Page 71)

Table 4. "A Meaning-Producing, Data-Driven and Human-Focused Digital Brand Ecosystem" (Page 81)

Table 5. "Contents, Purposes, Samples" (Page 93)

Contents

PART 1: BRAND STRATEGY, IMAGE, AND CONSUMER PERCEPTION

PART 2: BRAND STRATEGIES AND TRANSFORMATION OF BRAND IMAGE IN THE DIGITAL WORLD

BRAND IMAGE AND BRAND MANAGEMENT IN THE DIGITAL WORLD
Ahmet Cimer
2025

In this book, the brand is not treated merely as a commercial identity or visual symbol, but as a dynamic system integrating elements of meaning, perception, trust, and interaction. The emotional and cognitive bond a brand forms with consumers, and its decisive role in shaping purchasing behavior, constitute the foundational premise of this research.

The primary objective of this research and study is to examine the interaction between brand image, consumer perception, and purchasing behavior from a multidimensional perspective, and particularly to highlight the transformative impact of digital transformation on this relationship. In this context, the study evaluates the transition from traditional brand strategies to new strategic approaches in digital ecosystems within a theoretical and practical framework. Thus, this study may serve as a source of ideas for finding a way or method to compete with next-generation businesses that are seriously investing and operating in this field.

In the initial chapters, concepts such as brand equity, awareness, associations, perceived quality, and loyalty are discussed on a theoretical basis; the brand equity models of pioneering researchers like Aaker (1991) and Keller (1993) are examined in detail. This section clearly emphasizes that a brand is not just a communication tool but also an active element in consumers' identity construction and value perception.

In subsequent chapters, the effects of digitalization on brand management are assessed; next-generation approaches such as data-driven strategies, social media interactions, digital communities, and user experience management are detailed. In this process, phenomena like omnichannel marketing, personalized experiences, digital brand personality, content marketing, and user-generated content (UGC) are supported by case analyses to demonstrate their reinforcing and transformative effects on brand image.

The findings of the research reveal that brands must develop a holistic strategy based on the triad of trust, consistency, and meaning to achieve sustainable competitive advantage in the digital age. Today's consumers engage not only with product or service quality but also with the values a brand represents, its ethical stance, and its societal contributions.

In conclusion, this study aims to contribute to both academic literature and industry practice. It offers an opportunity to understand how concepts established in academia manifest in the real sector and business life. By addressing the new paradigms of branding in the digital world through a conceptual, analytical, and applied framework, it provides a strategic guide for businesses to build deeper, trust-based, and meaningful relationships with consumers.

Keywords: Brand Image, Consumer Perception, Digital Brand Management, Omni-Channel, Trust, Meaningful Branding, Brand Loyalty, Perceived Quality.

ABSTRACT

BRAND IMAGE AND BRAND MANAGEMENT IN THE DIGITAL WORLD

Ahmet Cimer 2025

This book approaches the concept of the brand not merely as a commercial identity or a visual symbol, but as a dynamic system in which meaning, perception, trust, and interaction are integrated. The emotional and cognitive bond that a brand establishes with the consumer constitutes the fundamental premise of this research, as it plays a decisive role in shaping purchasing behavior.

The primary aim of this research is to examine—through a multidimensional lens—the interplay among brand image, consumer perception, and purchasing behavior, while uncovering how digital transformation is reshaping that relationship. Accordingly, the study assesses the shift from traditional branding strategies to new strategic approaches within digital ecosystems, integrating theoretical and practical perspectives. Thus, this study can spark ideas on how to compete with a new generation of businesses that are seriously investing in this area.

In the initial sections, the concepts of brand equity, awareness, associations, perceived quality, and loyalty are discussed within a theoretical foundation, with detailed reference to the pioneering brand equity models of Aaker (1991) and Keller (1993). This section emphasizes that a brand is not merely a communication tool but also an active element in the construction of consumer identity and the formation of value perception.

In the subsequent sections, the effects of digitalization on brand management are examined in depth. Data-driven strategies, social media interactions, digital communities, and user experience management are analyzed as components of next-generation brand strategies. Within this framework, the impact of concepts such as omni-channel marketing, personalized experiences, digital brand personality, content marketing, and user-generated content (UGC) on brand image is supported by real-world case analyses.

The research findings indicate that in the digital age, brands must develop a holistic strategic framework built on trust, consistency, and meaning to achieve sustainable competitive advantage. Modern consumers form relationships not just through product or service quality, but also through the values, ethical stance, and social contributions a brand represents.

In conclusion, this study aims to bridge academic theory and business practice, contributing to both scholarly literature and industry applications. It offers insights into how academic concepts manifest in real-world business environments. By examining digital-era branding paradigms through conceptual, analytical, and practical lenses, the study serves as a strategic guide for businesses seeking to build deeper, trust-based, and meaning-driven consumer relationships.

Keywords: Brand Image, Consumer Perception, Digital Brand Management, Omni-Channel, Trust, Meaningful Branding, Brand Loyalty, Perceived Quality.

PART 1

BRAND STRATEGY, BRAND IMAGE, AND CONSUMER PERCEPTION

CHAPTER 1

INTRODUCTION, PURPOSE AND SIGNIFICANCE OF TOPIC

1. INTRODUCTION

Brand image and consumer perception are among the most debated and researched topics in contemporary marketing science. These concepts have become strategic elements that directly affect a company's success, especially in today's market conditions where competition is intensifying and consumer preferences are rapidly changing. Merely producing a product or offering a service no longer guarantees success. Beyond the product's physical existence, how it is positioned in the consumer's mind—that is, the brand and brand image that constitute the product's identity—often carries more meaning than the product itself.

The factors determining consumers' brand preferences are not limited to the product's technical specifications or price. Factors such as the story behind the product, brand values, communication style, and how it is perceived in society play important roles in today's consumer's decision-making process. In this context, modern marketing understanding focuses not only on the product's rational benefits but also on the psychological, symbolic, and emotional effects it creates in the consumer. Brand image, in this regard, plays a strategic role as an expression of the holistic perceptions and associations a brand creates in the consumer's mind.

Brand image extends beyond being merely an impression formed in the consumer's mind; it is directly related to a company's corporate reputation, market positioning, and customer loyalty. When making purchasing decisions, consumers consider not only the functionality of the product or service but also the emotional connection they establish with the brand, the values the brand represents, and the sense of identity the brand provides them. At this point, consumer perception is a psychological process in which the individual subjectively processes and makes sense of information from the external world. When a consumer looks at a brand, they consider not only the product's external form but also the experience the brand offers them, the image it creates in their imagination, and how they will be perceived in their social environment.

The relationship between brand image and consumer perception is not a linear, one-way connection; rather, it's a dynamic process that evolves through mutual interaction. While a consumer's past experiences, social environment, media messages, and personal values shape their perceptions of a brand, the brand's marketing strategies, communication style, and value propositions also guide the formation of these perceptions. Therefore, brand image is shaped not only by a company's planned communication efforts but also by the consumer's personal perceptual world.

In this study, the concepts of brand image and consumer perception will be explained in detail within a theoretical framework, followed by an examination of how these two concepts influence consumer purchasing behavior. Alongside fundamental theoretical approaches in the literature, current academic research will be analyzed to reveal the multidimensional nature of this relationship. Additionally, to provide a practical perspective, case studies of successful brands from various industries will be included. Through these cases, it will be explained with concrete examples how brand image becomes established in the consumer's mind, how this image influences consumer decision processes, and how it is reflected in marketing strategies.

In this context, the primary purpose of the study is to holistically reveal how brand image shapes consumer perception, how this perception influences consumer purchasing behavior, and ultimately how it guides companies' brand management strategies. The study aims to contribute to academic literature while also providing guiding insights for practitioners. Furthermore, by emphasizing the importance of developing consumer-focused marketing strategies, it argues that brands establishing effective communication with their target audience will create long-term competitive advantages.

1.1. Research Topic

This study aims to examine the impact of brand image on consumer purchasing behavior through a multidimensional approach. It provides an analysis centered on key questions such as how consumers form brand perceptions, what values and meanings a brand represents in their minds, and how these perceptions guide consumer preferences and purchase decisions. Starting from the premise that brand image is not merely a corporate-communication tool but also a force that shapes consumers' psychological, emotional, and social dispositions, the study scrutinizes the links among consumers' attitudes toward the brand, their perceptual assessments, and their behavioral responses.

Based on a literature review, the study surveys well-established theoretical approaches in marketing and consumer-behavior research and juxtaposes them with contemporary consumer trends. It also analyzes how brand image is manifested and applied across various industries, showing how the theoretical framework can be integrated with practical realities. Case studies from the food, technology, fashion, and service sectors concretize how brand image affects consumer behavior and allow us to assess whether this influence differs across industries.

In this context, the research aims to clarify both the causal and strategic relationship between brand image and consumer purchasing behavior. It also provides a comprehensive analysis that evaluates the holistic impact of brand image on modern consumer behavior, taking into account cultural, psychological, and digital transformation factors that influence this relationship.

1.2. Purpose and Significance of the Research

The central aim of this research, as discussed in this section, is to examine—in both theoretical and practical terms—how brand image influences consumer purchasing behavior. The study first analyzes how the literature treats these two concepts (brand image and consumer behavior) and then systematically evaluates existing theoretical approaches. The study will undertake a detailed analysis of how brand image shapes consumer perception, how that perception translates into the purchase process, and how it directs brand loyalty, trust, and preferences.

A further objective is to reveal the practical side of the issue by weaving theoretical insights together with real-life cases. To that end, brand-image reflections across the food, fashion, technology, and service sectors are analyzed through selected brands, illustrating how similar or divergent dynamics produce effects in different industries. This approach goes beyond pure theory and offers a multidimensional assessment that considers the sectoral, cultural, and strategic layers of the bond between brands and consumers.

The research also aims to address the fragmentation observed in academic studies on brand image and integrate diverse perspectives into a unified framework. It adopts an interdisciplinary approach, particularly examining how brand image is associated not only with marketing communication but also with consumer psychology, digital interactions, and sociocultural contexts. Thus, this study seeks to provide conceptual clarity in academia while serving as a guiding document for practitioners.

Additionally, the study aims to contribute to the development of new research questions in brand management and consumer behavior by providing a theoretical foundation for future qualitative and quantitative field research. In this regard, the research is designed not merely to synthesize existing knowledge but to foster new perspectives as a substantive academic contribution.

1.3. Scope of the Study

This book examines the relationship between brand image and consumer perception and purchasing behavior through a multidimensional lens. Grounded in both theoretical and practical approaches, the research systematically investigates how brand image is formed in the consumer's mind, the effects it exerts on decision-making processes, and the resulting implications for marketing strategy. The scope encompasses how brand image is perceived at cognitive, emotional, and behavioral levels; the conditions under which these perceptions translate into purchase behavior; and how cross-industry differences shape this process.

The study's scope extends beyond the basic definition and components of brand image to encompass its interplay with individual consumer perceptions, social influences, digital-media dynamics, competitive industry conditions, and cultural context. Consumers' brand perceptions, emotional attachments, and the impact of brand communication are assessed holistically.

In this context, the scope of the research encompasses the following key areas:

Examination of theoretical models linking brand image and consumer perception: The analysis details how brand image forms in the consumer's mind, interacts with individual perceptual processes, and can be explained by leading theoretical frameworks. Specifically, it elucidates the multidimensional structure of brand image through Keller's Customer-Based Brand Equity (CBBE) Model, Aaker's Brand Identity Approach, Kapferer's Brand Identity Prism, and Schmitt's Experiential Marketing Theory. Through these models, it is demonstrated how the image is shaped by various components such as mental representations, associations, symbolic values, and brand personality.

Systematic analysis of key theoretical approaches and current academic literature:

By reviewing literature published at national and international levels, studies addressing the relationship between brand image and consumer behavior have been comprehensively classified. Within this scope, methodological diversity, types of analysis used, sample structures, and findings have been evaluated in light of information obtained from both classical and contemporary academic sources. Thus, a synthesis of the current state of the literature has been created, strengthening the theoretical foundations of the research.

Evaluation of theory's practical reflections through sector-level case analyses: The impact of brand image on consumer behavior has been examined through case studies of selected brands from various sectors such as food, technology, fashion, and automotive. In this context, the image management strategies of globally active brands like Apple, McDonald's, Zara, and Volvo have been analyzed, and the effects of these strategies on consumer loyalty, brand trust, perceived brand value, price sensitivity, and repurchase intention have been assessed. Additionally, the role of elements such as digital marketing tools, corporate social responsibility practices, and sustainability communication in shaping brand image has been addressed in the case analyses.

An assessment of how consumer behaviors are shaped by brand image perception:

Consumer behavior is not solely based on rational evaluations; it is also influenced by emotional, social, cultural, and psychological factors. In this study, consumers' responses to brand image, the symbolic meanings evoked by the image, the emotional bond with the brand, trust relationships, and perceived value components have been analyzed in detail. Additionally, the study covers how digitalization shapes consumer-brand interactions through digital touchpoints such as social media, online user reviews, and influencer marketing. In this context, consumer experience has been re-evaluated in light of the digital age's transformative impact on brand image.

Overall, this study is a comprehensive, multidimensional research project that aims to understand brand image's reflection in consumer perception—both at a theoretical level and through industry representations. This approach to understanding brand image's impact on consumer decision-making mechanisms not only offers academic contributions but also strives to generate high-value practical insights for marketing managers, strategy developers, and brand professionals. Accordingly, this thesis serves as a guide that enhances conceptual depth in brand management while bridging theory and practice through industry case analyses.

CHAPTER 2

THE CONCEPT OF BRAND AND BRAND IMAGE

This section focuses on the concept of 'brand,' one of the foundational elements of marketing, and 'brand image,' the perceptual reflection it creates in consumers' minds. A brand is not merely a name or symbol but a multifaceted communication tool that establishes emotional, symbolic, and functional connections between producers and consumers. As both an expression of producer identity and a factor influencing consumer choice, brands have existed in various forms throughout history.

The earliest traces of branding date back to ancient times. Notably, artisans in Mesopotamia, Ancient Egypt, and Rome sought to distinguish their products by adding stamps or symbols, creating unique identities. These early examples demonstrate that brands were not just economic tools but also indicators of quality, responsibility, and ownership (Moore & Reid, 2008). During the Middle Ages, guild systems employed specific symbols for branding, allowing consumers to identify a product's origin, maker, and quality.

In its modern sense, the concept of branding began taking shape in marketing during the late 19th century with the rise of mass production and packaged goods. By the second half of the 20th century, brands evolved beyond mere identifiers of products or services into strategic tools shaping consumer perception. The American Marketing Association (AMA) defines a brand as 'a name, term, sign, symbol, or design or a combination of them intended to identify the goods or services of one seller or group of sellers and to differentiate them from competitors.' However, this definition acknowledges that a brand encompasses not just physical or visual elements but also emotional and psychological dimensions.

At this point, the concept of brand image representing the abstract and perceptual dimension of a brand comes to the forefront. Brand image is the totality of impressions, associations, and experiences that a consumer forms about a brand in their mind. Keller (1993) defines brand image as the set of perceptions and associations linked to a brand that reside in consumers' memory. In other words, brand image is shaped less by the product's physical attributes and more by the thoughts, feelings, and experiences the consumer associates with the brand.

Brand image forms the foundation of the relationship between a consumer and a brand, and this relationship is typically built on emotional rather than rational grounds. When consumers connect with brands, they place significant importance not only on functional benefits but also on symbolic meanings such as social status, personal expression, belonging, and lifestyle. Consequently, a strong brand image enhances consumer loyalty, reduces price sensitivity, and significantly increases the likelihood of being chosen over competing brands.

In conclusion, brand and brand image are viewed as two inseparable core concepts in contemporary marketing. While the brand marks the starting point of the relationship with the consumer, brand image is a key factor determining the depth, continuity, and direction of that relationship. Therefore, the branding process must strategically emphasize not only visual identity elements but also the image formed in the consumer's mind.

2.1. The Evolution and Importance of the Brand Concept

At its most basic, a brand is a name, term, sign, symbol, design, or combination thereof that identifies a product, service, or company and distinguishes it from competitors (Kotler & Keller, 2016). Today, however, the concept has moved beyond being a mere physical marker; it has become a bundle of perceptions, emotions, experiences, and promises lodged in the consumer's mind.

In other words, a brand is:

a- A set of values formed in the consumer's mind,

b- It is the entire set of meanings and associations attributed to a product or service.

c- And also a relationship of emotional attachment and trust.

A brand is not just a product; it is an experience that resides in the consumer's mind and heart. Brand management aims to create value on both rational and emotional levels. Therefore, in today's competitive environment, a brand is one of a company's most valuable assets.

The historical roots of branding reach back to the Middle Ages and even to ancient times. In the past, people used brands to show what they owned and who produced it. Branding practices are said to have existed in ancient Rome. In early medieval Europe protected brands appeared, and from the 13th century on they were regulated by decrees. At first the collective marks of guilds were protected, then individual marks. In France, names placed on manufactured goods in 1824 were later formalised under the Factory and Trade Mark Laws of 1857.

In the 19th century, American livestock farmers branded their animals with unique marks to prevent them from getting mixed up in pastures and markets. The modern concept of product branding and the use of brand names emerged in the 19th century. With the Industrial Revolution, advertising and marketing techniques evolved, making it crucial to present products and services under brand names.

In Anatolia, the notion of branding began when coppersmiths engraved their names and the day's date on copper items, and when carpet-weavers wove their names into carpets. The 1857 Regulation on Distinctive Marks stayed in force and served as the basis until the adoption of Trademark Law No. 551.

In today's business world, the most valuable asset is the brand. It creates demand, motivates employees, gives partners confidence, and convinces the financial community. In a rapidly globalising world, when entering a market, the product's brand, image, positioning, marketing strategy, advertising strategy, personality, message, and logo come to the fore. Muhtar Kent, Chairman and CEO of The Coca-Cola Company, said: 'A brand is a promise. But a good brand is a promise kept. Keeping the promise is what makes a good brand. You have to keep that promise every hour, every day, every week, every year. That is what matters. In any success story, the most important thing for staying power is not keeping it once or twice, but whether you can keep it all the time.'

In our country, the importance of branding has only recently been understood; awareness has grown with the new trademark laws introduced in the 1990s. The rise in trademark registrations is evidence of this. Therefore the 'Turquality' programme, launched in 2006 to create global brands from Turkey, was designed as a brand-development initiative with the vision of establishing ten global brands in ten years. Turquality—the first programme of its kind in the world—aims to become a brand reference in consumers' eyes and a catalyst for Turkish brands. Today, hundreds of brands from diverse sectors are supported under this program.

Being a brand holds great significance for businesses. Brands form a crucial strategy in ensuring a company's continuity. We can outline the importance of brands for businesses as follows. (Brand Management and Brand Strategies, Mehmet Akif Çakırer)

1. A brand is a company's tool for differentiation.
2. If the company behind a brand has a long-standing history, the brand carries the weight of that legacy.
3. A brand has financial value. Especially in manufacturing societies, a brand constitutes a significant portion of a company's total value. Additionally, companies with high brand value also have high stock market value.
4. A brand is a company's signature on its product and is responsible for representing the company in the best possible way. Therefore, it is essential to properly establish brand identity, protect it legally, and invest in the brand.
5. Because unknown brands pose a risk for distributors.

6. Brands also hold significant value from a human resources perspective. Working for a well-known brand is an important motivating factor for employees.

2.2.   Brand Image: Definition and Components

Brand image and consumer perception are two critically important concepts in modern marketing and consumer behavior literature. Brand image can be defined as the overall impression and perceptions consumers form about a brand in their minds. This image is shaped by consumers' direct or indirect interactions with the brand, their experiences, beliefs, and emotions about it. Consumer perception, on the other hand, refers to how individuals interpret marketing messages and product information—the process of making raw data meaningful. Consumers receive, select, and interpret various cues about a brand's products or services (e.g., advertisements, packaging, price, store environment) through their senses, thereby developing a personal perception of the brand . (en.wikipedia.org)

The relationship between brand image, consumer perception, and purchasing behavior is decisive for the success of marketing strategies. When consumers perceive a brand image positively, it can foster trust, loyalty, and higher purchase intent. Conversely, a negative brand image can breed distrust and drive consumers toward rival brands. In today's competitive markets, a strong and distinctive brand image is the only way to stand out among similar products and services. Indeed, a unique brand image differentiates the brand from competitors, making it more recognizable and appealing to consumers. Therefore, companies use perception management techniques to create and maintain their desired brand image in consumers' minds.en.wikipedia.orgen.wikipedia.org

Brand image is the totality of the associations, reputation, emotions, and impressions a brand evokes in consumers' minds. It emerges from the interplay of several key components:

1. **Functional Associations (Product Features and Performance):** The physical and functional attributes of the product or service the brand offers. Elements such as quality, durability, safety, and ease of use form the basis of these associations. (Keller and Aaker)

2. **Symbolic Values and Identity (Social Status and Self-Expression):** A brand can confer a lifestyle or social status upon the consumer. People select certain brands to express who they are.

   Example: Apple users = Innovative and modern lifestyle.

3. **Emotional Connections:** A brand should appeal to the consumer' s emotions. Emotional responses like trust, happiness, nostalgia, and love strengthen brand image.

Example: Coca-Cola = Happiness, a sense of togetherness with family.

4. **Cultural and Value-Based Image:** The brand's alignment with society's cultural values and norms. Associating it with values such as social-responsibility initiatives and environmental awareness.

   Example: Patagonia = Eco-friendly brand perception.

5. **Visual and Verbal Communication Elements:** Visual and verbal components like logos, color palettes, slogans, and packaging design. They embody brand identity and reinforce mental associations.

   Example: McDonald's "Golden Arches" – evokes speed, fun, and accessibility.

6. **Consumer Experiences:** The consumer's direct interactions with the brand (purchasing, usage, customer service, etc.). Positive experiences strengthen brand image; negative ones can weaken it. Example: Amazon = Fast delivery and easy return experience.

2.3. The Formation Process of Brand Image

Brand image isn't built overnight. It gradually takes shape through multiple interactions and experiences consumers have with the brand over time. This process unfolds through the following steps:

1. **Initial Contact and Awareness:** When a consumer first encounters the brand (through ads, social media, product displays, etc.), they form their initial impression. At this stage, the brand name, logo, colors, and slogans play a crucial role.

Example: Seeing a BMW logo on a billboard evokes the association of a "prestige car."

2. **Information Gathering and Perception Development:** The consumer begins to gather more information about the brand—common sources include ads, online reviews, social media content, and friend recommendations. This information starts shaping the consumer's initial perceptions of the brand.

3. **Experience and Interaction:** The consumer directly experiences the brand—purchasing and using the product, contacting customer service, or experiencing the store atmosphere. If the experiences are positive, brand perception strengthens; if negative, a poor image can take hold.

4. **Building Associations:** Based on experiences and information, the consumer forms mental associations with the brand:

- o   Functional (high-quality, practical)

- o   Emotional (sincere, fun)

- o   Symbolic (prestigious, youthful)

Example: Apple = Innovation + Creativity + High status.

5. **Attitude Formation:** *The consumer develops an attitude toward the brand:*

Positive attitude → Loyalty and repeat-purchase behavior

Negative attitude → Switching to alternative brands

6. **Image Consolidation:** Continuous positive touchpoints and consistent communication make the brand image enduring over time. Every new experience with the brand either reinforces or erodes the existing image.

The concept of "brand image" is often contrasted with brand identity in the marketing literature. Brand identity is the image the firm intends to create and communicate for its brand, whereas brand image is the image consumers actually perceive. In other words, brand identity is what the company controls (logo, design, tone of voice, etc.), while brand image is the resulting perception in consumers' minds. For example, a company may position its brand as innovative and high-quality (brand identity); if consumers actually perceive it that way, a positive brand image has been formed.en.wikipedia.org

2.4. Types of Brand Image

Brand image is categorized into different types based on how it is perceived in consumers' minds and which aspects of the brand are emphasized. Each type offers consumers a distinct value, message, and feeling. Here are the fundamental types of brand image:

1. **Functional Image:** An image built on tangible product/service attributes such as quality, performance, durability, and value for money. Consumers evaluate it rationally. (David A. Aaker, Building Strong Brands, 1996; Kevin L. Keller, Conceptualizing, Measuring and Managing Customer-Based Brand Equity, 1993)

   Example: Toyota = Reliability and long-lasting vehicles.

2. **Symbolic Image (Status & Identity):** The brand confers identity, social status, and a sense of belonging. Consumers use it to express who they are or who they aspire to be. (David A. Aaker, Building Strong Brands, 1996 – Kevin L. Keller, Conceptualizing, Measuring and Managing Customer-Based Brand Equity, 1993)

   Example: Rolex = A symbol of prestige and luxury status.

3. **Emotional Image:** This refers to the brand's image based on the emotional responses it evokes in consumers, such as trust, happiness, nostalgia, comfort, and similar feelings. Consumers connect with the brand more through their emotions than rational reasons. (David A. Aaker, Building Strong Brands, 1996 – Kevin L. Keller, Conceptualizing, Measuring and Managing Customer-Based Brand Equity, 1993)

   Example: Coca-Cola = Happiness and a sense of sharing.

4. **Corporate Image:** This is the perception of the company or institution behind the brand in the eyes of consumers. Elements such as social responsibility, ethical values, and environmental awareness shape this image. (Kapferer, J.N., New Strategic Brand Management, 2008)

   Example: Patagonia = Perceived as an eco-friendly, ethically producing company.

5. **Relational Image (Customer Experience Image):** This is the image based on the one-on-one relationship the consumer establishes with the brand, influenced by experiences such as customer service quality, post-sale support, and personalization. A good relationship enhances loyalty, while a poor one damages the image.

(Hollebeek, L.D. & Chen T, Exploring Customer Brand Engagement, 2014)

Example: Amazon = A fast and seamless shopping experience.

6. **Social Image:** This is tied to how the individual is perceived by their social circle through the brand. People also care about how others view them via the brand.

   Example: Tesla = The image of an innovative, eco-conscious, and visionary individual.

A brand doesn't just sell products—it also offers emotion, identity, connection, and value. This is why brands must strategically build different types of images.

2.5. Brand Image Management and Strategic Approaches

This topic requires addressing both headings separately, examining them in detail, gaining a thorough understanding, and evaluating them.

2.5.1. Brand Image Management

Brand image management is the deliberate set of activities aimed at creating, developing, and maintaining the desired perception of a brand in the consumer's mind. The primary goal of this process is to create a strong, consistent, and positive impression in consumer perception while clearly communicating the brand's values, identity, and promises.

Brand image management isn't just about creating an initial perception—it also involves preserving, enhancing, and, when necessary, repositioning that perception over time. Among the core principles of brand image management, we can highlight the following concepts:

1. **Consistency:** Brand messaging must be coherent across all communication channels (advertising, social media, product experience).

2. **Emotional Connection:** A brand must occupy not just a mental space but also an emotional one in the consumer's mind.

3. **Perception Management:** Consumer perceptions of the brand should be regularly measured and interventions made when necessary. Leaving processes to unfold without monitoring will directly impact the effectiveness of strategies and plans, determining whether they work as intended.

4. **Innovation and Renewal:** Flexibility must be shown to adapt to changing consumer expectations. Today, time moves incredibly fast and the pace of change has reached

unprecedented levels. In this regard, innovation and renewal of the brand and its products are crucial for promptly responding to consumer expectations.

5. **Crisis Preparedness:** Plans should be made in advance for image-damaging crises, and rapid, transparent communication strategies must be developed. This is of critical importance. Having pre-prepared plans will give us the opportunity to take swift action against negative events.

At the core of brand image lie the associations consumers hold about the brand. According to researchers like Keller (1993), brand image is the sum of perceptions and associations consumers mentally link to a brand. These associations encompass both functional and emotional elements—such as product quality, reliability, prestige, user experience, and symbolic value—as we've previously noted.

For example, the immediate association of safety when 'Volvo' is mentioned, or the evocation of refreshment and tradition when 'Coca-Cola' is heard, illustrate how brand image works. Therefore, when managing brand image, the product offered to the market and the brand must be evaluated within the framework of the principles mentioned above and must be consistent with each other.

2.5.2. Strategic approaches

Because brand image management is an extremely delicate issue, it must be developed within a specific systematic framework and with strategic approaches that allow progress without harming the product or brand or tarnishing the image. Here, different concepts will help us define our strategy:

1. **Positioning Strategy:** The brand works on its identity and differentiating attributes to occupy a specific place in the consumer's mind. Effective positioning ensures the brand stands out clearly among competitors.

   Example: Volvo = "The safest car."

2. **Value Proposition:** Brand image is the sum of all tangible and intangible benefits that a brand offers to the consumer. This proposition forms the core of the brand image.

   Example: Dove = "Championing real beauty."

3. **Emotional Branding:** Aims to increase brand loyalty by forging emotional connections with consumers. In highly competitive environments, emotional bonds can outweigh rational benefits.

   Example: Coca-Cola = "Sharing happiness."

4. **Experiential Marketing:** Every lived experience with the brand directly shapes its image. Store design, customer-

service quality, packaging experience, and similar elements are managed within this scope.

Example: Apple Stores = "A temple to the tech experience."

5. **Social Responsibility and Reputation Management:** Brands build a strong public image through social responsibility initiatives. Environmental awareness and community contribution projects enhance brand reputation.

   Example: Patagonia = "Environmentally conscious production."

6. **Image Repositioning:** Faced with shifting market dynamics or an image crisis, a brand enters a process of strategically changing how it is perceived.

   Example: Burberry = Transforming from a traditional "old-fashioned" image into a youthful, luxury fashion brand.

Effective brand image management enhances brand loyalty, reduces price sensitivity, enables premium pricing, increases customer lifetime value, provides a competitive edge, and makes brand reputation more resilient during crises. Brand image management isn't just about advertising. It's a process of building an emotional and mental connection with consumers across all brand touchpoints over time.

A strong brand image offers significant advantages in the marketplace. First, a positive brand image builds consumer trust. Consumers rely on their perceived image of the brand, which triggers repeat purchases and loyalty behaviors. For example, a brand with a high-quality image fosters trust among consumers, strengthening customer retention. Second, a strong image enables brand differentiation. Even when competing products have similar features, a brand's perceived image can influence consumer preference.en.wikipedia.orgen.wikipedia.org

Especially in product categories with numerous similar brands, consumers often make choices based on their perceived image. Lastly, brand image is a critical component of brand equity. Brands with a positive image can hold higher value in consumers' eyes and enjoy greater pricing flexibility; consumers may willingly pay slightly higher prices for brands they trust and love.

CHAPTER 3

CONSUMER BEHAVIOR AND THE PURCHASE PROCESS

In modern marketing, the concept of consumer behavior must be thoroughly examined, with emphasis on its impact on purchase processes. Brand, brand image, perception, consumer behavior, and purchasing are interconnected processes in constant interaction. To clarify, these processes need to be explored in greater depth.

3.1. Definition and Key Elements of Consumer Behavior

Consumer behavior encompasses all mental, emotional, and physical activities individuals or groups exhibit in acquiring, using, and disposing of products, services, ideas, or experiences to fulfill their needs and desires (Schiffman & Wisenblit, 2019).

In other words, consumer behavior is a multi-stage decision and action process that begins before purchase, continues through usage, and concludes post-consumption. During this process, consumers gather information, evaluate options, make decisions, purchase, use, assess, and sometimes return or recommend products. Key factors shaping consumer behavior include psychological, personal, sociocultural, situational, and marketing elements.

3.2. Psychological Factors in Consumer Behavior

Psychological factors play a central role in understanding consumer behavior. Purchase decisions aren't shaped solely by external stimuli or economic conditions; they're also directly influenced by an individual's internal cognitive processes, emotional states, and mental tendencies. Psychological factors determine how consumers perceive a product, develop attitudes toward it, and navigate mental processes during decision-making. Below are the four most widely accepted core psychological factors:

1. Motivation: The Driving Force Behind Purchase Desire

Motivation is an internal drive that compels individuals to perform specific behaviors. When consumers recognize a need, they become motivated to fulfill it. Maslow's hierarchy of needs is frequently referenced in this context. According to Maslow, individuals tend to prioritize physiological needs first, then move toward higher-level needs such as safety, belonging, esteem, and self-actualization. A consumer's decision to purchase a luxury car may not stem solely from a transportation need; prestige, social status, or self-esteem needs could also trigger this motivation. Thus, motivation is one of the fundamental psychological dynamics underlying consumer behavior.

2. Perception: The Selective Mental Process for Information

Perception is the process by which individuals select, organize, and interpret stimuli from their environment. Two different consumers exposed to the same product may perceive it in vastly different ways. This demonstrates that perception is shaped by subjective interpretations rather than objective reality. Factors influencing perception include prior experiences, individual attitudes, cultural background, brand awareness, and media influence. For example, one consumer might perceive a prestigious brand's product as higher quality, while another might view the same product as an overpriced status symbol. Therefore, how brands are positioned in consumers' minds holds strategic importance for perception management.

3. Learning: How Experiences Influence Decision-Making

Learning is the process by which individuals acquire knowledge through experiences and develop behavior patterns based on that knowledge. When a consumer has a positive experience with a product or brand, they store this experience in their mental memory and tend to gravitate toward that brand in similar need situations. Classical conditioning (Pavlov), operant conditioning (Skinner), and cognitive learning theories are widely used to explain learning processes in consumer behavior. For instance, loyalty cards, promotions, and positive brand experiences serve as tools for fostering brand loyalty through learning.

4. Attitudes and Beliefs: Cognitive and Emotional Responses to Brands

Attitudes are relatively enduring emotional and cognitive tendencies that individuals develop toward an object, brand, or product. Beliefs, on the other hand, form the cognitive foundation of these attitudes. If a consumer holds a positive attitude toward a brand, this can directly increase their purchase intent. For example, if a consumer believes 'Brand X produces eco-friendly products,' this belief can translate into a positive attitude and, over time, brand loyalty. Changing attitudes is a challenging process; thus, brands must prioritize developing content aimed at forming or reinforcing attitudes in their communication strategies.

In conclusion, psychological elements form the cognitive foundation of consumer behavior. These factors are key variables that must be considered when crafting marketing strategies. What motivates consumers, how they perceive, what they learn, and what they believe play decisive roles in shaping brand image and influencing purchase decisions.

3.3. Personal Factors in Consumer Behavior

One of the most significant variables influencing consumer behavior is an individual's personal characteristics. These traits are linked to their demographic, psychographic, and socioeconomic profile and can affect purchasing decisions both consciously and subconsciously. The personal attributes each individual possesses directly shape their needs, desires, value judgments, and purchasing patterns. Below are the key components of how personal factors influence consumer behavior:

1. Age and Life Stage

An individual's age and life stage throughout their lifecycle alter the nature of their needs and expectations. For instance, younger consumers tend to gravitate toward technology and trend-sensitive products, while older individuals may prioritize functionality and reliability. The product preferences and brand perceptions of a college student versus a parent with children can differ significantly. Additionally, the combination of 'lifestyle' and 'life stage' is one of the strategic variables brands consider when segmenting their target audiences.

2. Gender

Gender, both physiologically and socially, creates distinctions in consumer behavior. Male and female consumers often assign different values to the same product. For example, female consumers may prioritize aesthetics and detail, while male consumers might focus more on technical specifications and performance. While these differences evolve over time due to shifting gender roles and individual preferences, they remain a key segmentation criterion in marketing strategies.

3. Lifestyle

Lifestyle refers to behavioral patterns shaped by an individual's daily habits, social relationships, interests, values, and worldview. Even individuals of the same age, income group, and city may gravitate toward entirely different product categories if their lifestyles differ. The brands, products, and stores preferred by an athletic individual may vary drastically from those chosen by an intellectual. In marketing communication, 'lifestyle segmentation' is therefore a frequently applied targeting method.

4. Personality

Personality refers to an individual's relatively stable character traits, attitudes, and behavioral patterns. An extroverted, novelty-seeking, risk-taking consumer will show interest in different products than an introverted, traditional, and conservative one. Aaker's (1997) Brand Personality Model demonstrates that consumers tend to associate brands with their own personality traits. In this context, when alignment is achieved between consumer personality and brand personality, brand image becomes stronger and more enduring.

5. Income Level and Economic Status

Income level is a factor that directly influences a consumer's spending capacity and purchasing power. While individuals in high-income groups typically gravitate toward luxury, prestigious, and differentiated products, consumers in low-income groups tend to prefer price-sensitive, functional, and essential-needs products. However, income level doesn't just determine spending amounts—it also shapes spending patterns and value priorities. As a result, income segmentation plays a critical role in brands' pricing and product positioning strategies.

In conclusion, personal factors reflect the individual dimension of consumer behavior. Each person responds differently to brand images based on their age, lifestyle, personality, and economic status. This necessitates that brands adopt segmented strategies— rather than uniform ones—to appeal to different groups of individuals.

3.4. Sociocultural Elements in Consumer Behavior

Another factor shaping consumer behavior is the social and cultural environment in which an individual operates. A consumer is not just an independent decision-maker but also a person guided by collective norms, values, and social interactions as part of society. Consequently, consumption preferences often develop in alignment with social roles and cultural codes rather than personal traits. Sociocultural elements can be examined under three main headings:

1. Family: The Primary Shaper of Purchasing Behavior

Family is the first social structure where an individual's consumption habits take shape. Consumption patterns observed during childhood can leave lasting effects on the brand preferences and purchasing decisions a person develops later in life. Factors such as parents' brand loyalty, price sensitivity, and emphasis on quality in product selection serve as models for children. Additionally, among adults, roles within the family (e.g., the decision-making spouse, the child as a user, the parent as the purchaser) make the buying process multidimensional. Thus, family is a key driver of consumer behavior in both individual and collective decision-making contexts.

2. Reference Groups: Preferences Shaped by Social Interaction

Reference groups refer to communities an individual belongs to or aspires to join. Examples include friend circles, colleagues, social clubs, digital communities, or celebrity figures. Individuals may shape their purchasing decisions based on information and observations gained from these groups. Peer groups exert particularly strong influence on younger consumers. Additionally, influencers or opinion leaders followed on social media can function as reference groups, affecting brand image and purchasing tendencies. Such groups not only provide information to consumers but also impose normative pressure, dictating 'appropriate' consumption patterns.

3. Culture:

Societal Codes That Determine Consumption Practices

Culture encompasses a society's shared values, beliefs, norms, and symbolic structures. Consumption behaviors derive meaning within this cultural framework. The fact that owning the same product carries different meanings in different societies is a clear indicator of this phenomenon. For instance, Western societies place greater emphasis on individualism and innovation, while Eastern societies prioritize traditional values and social harmony. This cultural difference directly influences what consumers expect from a brand, how they perceive it, and the meanings they attach to it. Additionally, subcultures, ethnic groups, and regional lifestyles also contribute to diversity in consumption preferences. For brands operating in international markets, it is therefore essential to develop strategies that account for these cultural differences.

In conclusion, sociocultural elements are powerful factors that shape a consumer's identity, values, and social relationships. Ignoring these factors can hinder the establishment of the desired emotional and symbolic connection between a brand and its consumers. Therefore, when developing marketing strategies, the social structure and cultural background of the target audience must be thoroughly analyzed.

3.5.   Situational Factors in Consumer Behavior

Consumer purchasing behavior is shaped not only by an individual's intrinsic psychological or sociocultural traits but also by the contextual conditions in which the shopping occurs. In this context, situational factors refer to environmental and momentary influences on consumption decisions. Although purchasing is often a planned behavior, it can be altered by the impact of the surroundings. Thus, the same individual may react differently to the same product at different times and in different environments. Below, the influence of situational factors on consumer behavior is examined under three main headings:

1. Time of Purchase

The time frame in which a consumer seeks a product or service can directly influence the speed and nature of their purchasing behavior. Under time pressure, the decision-making process shortens, and the tendency to buy without detailed consideration increases. During special occasions like holiday seasons, New Year's, or Valentine's Day, emotional influences, gifting motivations, and promotional campaigns boost purchase frequency and spending. Additionally, in urgent-need shopping scenarios, brand loyalty may be lower, as consumers tend to gravitate toward readily available products. Thus, the psychological and behavioral effects of purchase timing cannot be overlooked.

2. Physical Environment

The physical or digital environment in which a consumer shops can significantly influence purchasing decisions. Store ambiance (lighting, music, scent, layout, color schemes) can evoke emotional responses, making the shopping experience more appealing or off-putting. Similarly, on e-commerce platforms, elements like site design, user experience (UX), visual quality, product descriptions, and ease of payment shape purchasing behavior. A positive shopping environment encourages consumers to spend more time in-store or online, increasing the likelihood of purchases.

Therefore, in-store experiences and online user interfaces are regarded as strategic tools for reinforcing brand image.

3. Current Mood

A consumer's emotional state during shopping is a significant psychological variable that influences product evaluations and decisions. While a happy individual views shopping as a means of reward and enjoyment, for a stressed or unhappy person, shopping may become a temporary escape or relaxation method. This situation can particularly increase impulsive buying behaviors. For example, research shows that stressed individuals are more inclined to shop, and this tendency can lead to unplanned purchasing decisions. Brands appealing to consumers' emotional states in advertising messages or store atmosphere is highly effective in creating emotional triggers during the decision-making process.

In conclusion, although situational factors often appear as short-term and external variables, they can have a decisive impact on consumer behavior. Marketing strategies that dynamically account for such immediate conditions can provide a significant advantage, especially in highly competitive industries.

3.6. Marketing Elements in Consumer Behavior

Consumer behavior is shaped not only by an individual's intrinsic traits or social environment but also by the guiding influence of marketing strategies. In modern marketing, consumer-centricity has become a fundamental principle; businesses tailor all their activities, from product development processes to promotion strategies, according to consumer expectations. In this context, the four core elements of the marketing mix—product, price, place (distribution), and promotion—have significant effects on consumer behavior.

1. Product: The Role of Quality, Design, and Functionality in Consumer Preference

A product represents the physical or service-based value offered to the consumer. Technical features, functionality, quality, packaging design, ease of use, and similar attributes directly determine consumer preference. Innovation stands out in technological products, design in aesthetic products, and quality and trust in food products. The product also serves as a carrier of brand image; a well-designed product can foster loyalty by increasing trust in the brand. Satisfaction based on consumer experiences further supports repeat purchase behavior.

2. Price: The Balance Between Perceived Value and Willingness to Pay

Price refers to the amount a consumer is willing to pay for a product or service. Pricing strategies directly influence how consumers position the product. Consumers interpret price not only as an economic cost but also as an indicator of perceived value. In this context, variables such as 'price sensitivity,' 'value orientation,' and 'price perception' come into play. A high price may be perceived positively as a quality indicator in some segments, while a low price may appeal to discount-focused consumers. Aligning pricing with consumer psychology in marketing strategies can be influential in purchase decisions.

3. Place (Distribution): Accessibility and Ease of Purchase

The channels through which a product reaches consumers are a critical factor influencing the quality of the shopping experience and the likelihood of purchase. Physical store locations, shelf arrangements, retail channels, e-commerce sites, and mobile apps serve as consumer touchpoints with the product. Easy accessibility accelerates the purchasing process and reduces barriers to purchase. Additionally, omnichannel distribution strategies enhance the experience by offering consumers flexibility and choice. Particularly in the post-pandemic era, online distribution channels have reshaped consumer habits.

4. Promotion: The Impact of Brand Messages on Behavior

Promotion encompasses all communication activities aimed at marketing a product or service. This includes advertisements, sales promotions, public relations campaigns, social media content, and direct marketing techniques. These tools help consumers learn about the product, remember it, form an emotional connection with the brand, and positively influence their purchasing decisions. Particularly in today's digital age, content marketing, influencer marketing, and user reviews have become decisive elements in promotion strategies.

CHAPTER 4

PURCHASING PROCESS AND STAGES

The purchasing process represents the entirety of the mental, emotional, and behavioral stages a consumer goes through before making a decision to buy a product or service. This process is not limited to the moment of purchase; it is a multi-stage decision chain involving pre- and post-purchase phases. Consumer behavior revolves around the purchasing decision, which matures through a series of stages. (Source: Schiffman & Wisenblit, 2019; Kotler & Keller, 2016)

The consumer purchasing process generally consists of five key stages:

1. **Need Recognition (Problem Identification):** The consumer perceives a gap between their current state and their desired state. This gap creates a need or desire. For example, a broken phone may trigger the need for a new one.

2. **Information Search:** The consumer begins gathering information about products/services that could fulfill their need. This involves internal sources (past experiences) and external sources (friend recommendations, online research, advertisements). For instance, comparing Apple vs. Samsung by reading reviews.

3. **Evaluation of Alternatives:** The consumer assesses the gathered information and compares various alternatives. Factors like price, quality, brand image, and features are considered. For example, iPhone 15 Pro vs. Galaxy S24 Ultra?

4. **Purchase Decision:** The consumer makes a choice among the alternatives and finalizes the purchase. However, environmental factors (peer influence, stock availability, instant promotions) may also influence the decision.

5. **Post-Purchase Behavior:** After using the product/service, the consumer evaluates whether they are satisfied with their decision. Satisfaction leads to loyalty and recommendations, while dissatisfaction drives complaints and the search for alternatives.

The purchasing process can be rational (conscious decisions) or emotional (decision-making based on feelings). Some purchases are routine (daily products), while others are complex (high-risk purchases like homes or cars). Digitalization has significantly accelerated the information search and evaluation stages. Purchasing is not an event but a process: a need arises, information is gathered, alternatives are evaluated, a decision is made, and an assessment follows. At each stage, brands aim to influence this process through their strategies.

4.1. Psychological and Social Factors Influencing Purchase Decisions

Individual mental processes play a significant role in consumers' purchase decisions. These processes determine how the consumer perceives, evaluates, and ultimately decides on a product. The primary psychological factors enabling purchase decisions include:

1. **Motivation:** The internal drive that compels a consumer to make a purchase. Basic needs (like water and food) form the first level of Maslow's hierarchy of needs. Beyond these, higher-level needs (such as prestige and esteem) occupy the upper tiers. For example, buying a luxury watch provides a sense of status.

2. **Perception:** The process by which an individual selects, organizes, and interprets information from their environment. Perception influences consumer behavior more than facts do. For instance, an 'Organic Product' label creates a perception of greater healthiness in the consumer.

3. **Learning:** The impact of past experiences and accumulated knowledge on purchase decisions. Successful product experiences encourage repeat purchases. For example, choosing the same car brand again after a satisfying experience is a common consumer behavior.

4. **Attitudes and Beliefs:** The emotional and cognitive tendencies a consumer holds toward a brand or product. Positive attitudes increase purchase likelihood, while negative attitudes reduce it. For example, the belief 'IKEA is eco-friendly due to its carbon-neutral success' is a positive attitude that drives purchase decisions.

Consumer purchase decisions are shaped not only by individual mental processes but also by environmental and social interactions. These include family, reference groups, social status, and culture/subcultures.

1. **Family:** It is the primary determinant of early consumption habits and brand preferences. Preferences learned from family during childhood can remain influential in adulthood. For example, if a family consistently consumes Ülker products, the individual may habitually prefer this brand.

2. **Reference Groups:** Reference group influence refers to the impact of social groups that an individual belongs to or aspires to join. Opinions from circles like friends, coworkers, or sports clubs can affect purchasing decisions. For example, if a friend group wears popular brands, there's a tendency to prefer those same brands.

3. **Social Status:** A consumer's position in society (social class)—influences brand and product choices. The desire for higher social status may lead to a preference for luxury and prestige products. Brands like BMW and Louis Vuitton serve as examples of status display.

4. **Culture and subcultures:** Culture and subcultures shape consumer preferences through a society's broader values, norms, and traditions. Individuals may also align with the norms of their subcultures (e.g., youth subculture, tech enthusiasts). For instance, someone in the vegan subculture may prefer vegan products.

Purchasing decisions arise from a complex interplay of individual psychological processes and societal influences. Successful brands must appeal to both the consumer's mind and their social environment

CHAPTER 5

THE IMPACT OF DIGITALIZATION ON CONSUMER BEHAVIOR

Digitalization is the process of integrating information technologies (internet, mobile devices, AI, social media, big data, etc.) into every aspect of daily life. Commerce, marketing, communication, and consumption habits have undergone radical changes as a result.

Digitalization hasn't just altered and accelerated consumer behavior—it has also sparked revolutionary transformations in fundamental areas like the purchasing process, perception management, and customer relations. Here are some key impacts of digitalization on post-digital consumer behavior:

1. **Instant Access to Information:** Consumers can now access information about products and brands anytime, anywhere. Product reviews, price comparisons, and user feedback directly influence purchasing decisions. For example, shoppers can now see a product in-store and check online reviews before deciding (a behavior known as showrooming).

2. **Empowered Consumers:** Consumers have become more informed and discerning. Rather than relying on traditional

ads, they base decisions on their own research and online experiences. For instance, reading hundreds of user reviews before purchasing helps consumers feel more confident and empowered.

3. **Omnichannel Shopping Experience:** Physical stores, websites, mobile apps, and social media platforms have become interconnected. Consumers research on one channel and purchase on another. For example, it's now possible to order a product online and pick it up in-store. This offers consumers greater convenience in comparing products and shopping with less time spent.

4. **Personalization Expectation:** Consumers expect tailored offers and experiences. AI and big data technologies enable personalized ads, product recommendations, and campaigns. For example, Spotify's weekly personalized playlists or Amazon's recommendation systems allow individuals to receive offers customized to their interests.

5. **Faster and Easier Purchasing:** Mobile payment systems (Apple Pay, Google Pay) and one-click shopping options have accelerated the purchasing process. Wait times have decreased, and buying decisions have become more

spontaneous. For instance, ordering food with a single click via an app.

6. **The Role of Social Media:** Consumer decisions are influenced by content seen on social media—influencer reviews, user experiences, and brand campaigns directly impact purchasing behavior. For example, buying a product promoted by an influencer on Instagram is now a common occurrence.

7. **Two-Way Communication in Consumer Relations:** While traditional ads involve one-way communication, brands and consumers constantly interact in the digital space. Consumers can directly ask questions, lodge complaints, or express satisfaction. For instance, engaging with brand customer service via Twitter speeds up communication and leads to more efficient and successful outcomes for both parties.

In this context:

1. **Digital Native:** Younger generation consumers inherently integrated into the digital world.

2. **Digital Immigrant:** Adult consumers who adapted to digitalization later in life.

3. **Social Consumer:** Consumers who rely on comments and shares in social networks when making decisions.

4. **Mobile Consumer:** User consumers who primarily shop via mobile devices and mobile channels.

This has given rise to different consumer typologies.

Digitalization has accelerated consumers' access to information, expanded their options, and made decision-making processes more personal and dynamic. Successful brands shape their marketing strategies by understanding these new expectations and behaviors of digital consumers. Advancing through digital channels has not only saved consumers time but also provided them with the opportunity to evaluate criteria such as price, quality, and brand simultaneously.

Research indicates that the volume of shopping through digital channels will increase significantly over the next 10 years. The global e-commerce market is projected to be worth approximately $21.6 trillion by 2025 and could reach $75 trillion by 2034, with an average annual growth rate of 14.9%

(www.precedenceresearch.com). According to Mordor Intelligence, e-commerce is expected to grow at an annual rate of 18.7% between 2025 and 2030.

CHAPTER 6

THE RELATIONSHIP BETWEEN BRAND IMAGE AND PURCHASE BEHAVIOR

Academic studies have examined the effects of brand image on consumers across various dimensions. For instance, external cues such as a brand's name and reputation have been found to significantly influence consumers' perception of quality ( ). A well-known and reputable brand name (e.g., a luxury brand logo) can lead to the same product being perceived as higher quality compared to unbranded or lesser-known brands. This demonstrates that consumers rely on brand image when making decisions, especially when they have limited information about the product.en.wikipedia.org

6.1. The Role of Brand Image on Consumer Perception

Perception, in psychology and cognitive sciences, refers to the reception, interpretation, selection, and organization of emotional information. It consists of signals in the nervous system generated by the physical stimulation of sensory organs.

Perception is the process of interpreting sensations and organizing them into meaningful forms. Information received through our five senses is interpreted and given meaning, allowing us to understand the external world. From a consumer behavior perspective, the concept of perception stands out as a factor in pre-purchase, during-purchase, and post-purchase interpretations (www.slideshare.net/slideshow, Prof. Dr. Suzan Çoban).

Perception management can be defined as the efforts of an organization or brand to shape and guide the perceptions of its target audiences (consumers, stakeholders, or the general public) about itself. Although the concept originated in military and political communication fields, it is now widely applied by businesses. In a marketing context, perception management involves planned communication strategies aimed at creating the desired brand image and correcting negative perceptions.(tr.wikipedia.org)

Perception management involves carefully crafting and delivering brand messages and images to target audiences, thereby embedding the desired brand perception in their minds. In the age of social media, the importance of perception management has grown significantly. On social platforms, perception management entails delivering tailored messages to target consumer groups through digital channels, guiding them toward desired behaviors aligned with their wants and needs. For example, a food company might share content that aligns with healthy living trends on social media to position itself as a "healthy and trustworthy" brand. This is a practical application of perception management: the goal is to establish an image in consumers' minds that associates the brand with healthy products.(tr.wikipedia.org)

Perception management is also closely tied to reputation management. Negative news or rumors about a brand can quickly skew consumer perception. In such cases, companies employ perception management strategies to rectify the situation: they take steps like apology campaigns, corrective advertisements, and public relations initiatives to repair the damaged image. For instance, when an automotive company has to issue a major recall due to a technical fault, it must use communication channels to reassure customers and manage perceptions by demonstrating its commitment to resolving the issue.

Perception management can also be leveraged to gain a competitive edge. Creating a perception that a brand is superior to its competitors can sway consumer preferences in its favor. To achieve this, companies may use advertising campaigns, comparative ads, or influencer collaborations. For example, a tech company might emphasize the innovative features of its products to foster a perception that competitors are "lagging behind." If successful, consumers will begin to view the brand as superior due to its innovative image.(tr.wikipedia.org)

Ultimately, perception management aims to align the image a brand projects with the perception formed in consumers' minds.

Companies maintain constant communication to bridge the gap between brand identity and brand image. Through consistent messaging, high-quality experiences, and swift crisis responses, consumer perception is managed to reinforce the desired brand image. To ensure the interaction between brand image (the perceptual impression left on consumers) and consumer perception (an individual's subjective evaluation of the brand), a brand must implement strategic and holistic communication management. This interaction is strengthened through the following methods. (en.wikipedia.org)

1. **Consistent Communication:** The brand must convey the same message and feeling across all touchpoints (advertising, social media, in-store experience, customer service). Consistency fosters a clear and reliable brand perception in consumers' minds.

2. **Emotional Connection:** Brands should offer not just products but meaning and value (e.g., freedom, security, prestige). When consumers form an emotional bond with a brand, perception deepens, and brand image strengthens.

3. **Experiential Marketing:** A brand's physical, digital, and service experiences should exceed consumer expectations and create positive memories. Favorable experiences

reinforce brand perception and solidify its mental representation.

4. **Social and Cultural Alignment:** Brand values should resonate with the social norms and cultural expectations of the target audience. When consumers identify with a brand, perception becomes stronger and more enduring.

5. **Continuous Feedback and Improvement:** Consumer perception can change over time. Brands should consistently measure perception through data analytics and customer feedback, making necessary adjustments.

In short, brand image shapes consumer perception when managed correctly. Over time, consumer perception reinforces and alters brand image. This relationship is an interactive cycle that, when managed well, fosters brand loyalty, trust, and value. In this reciprocal process, brand image influences consumer perception through "Communication, Experience, Values," while consumer perception, in turn, reshapes brand image through "Feedback and Adaptation."

6.2. The Impact of Brand Image on Purchase Decision-Making

Brand image encompasses all the perceptions, associations, experiences, and emotions a consumer holds about a brand. This image directly influences the consumer's purchase decision, whether consciously or intuitively.

When brand image is strong:

a- The perceived quality of the product/service increases,

b- Purchase risk decreases,

c- Brand loyalty and trust are established,

d- Consumer decision-making becomes faster and easier.

A weak or negative brand image, however:

a- It creates hesitation,

b- It increases the inclination toward alternative brands.

Brand image has distinct impacts at each stage of the purchase decision process. After a consumer recognizes their need, options with strong brand associations are the first to come to mind. For example, when thinking of sneakers, brands like Adidas or Nike immediately spring to mind.

Well-known brands attract more consumer attention during the information-gathering phase and may eliminate the need for extensive research due to the trust they inspire. For instance, a trusted brand like Samsung might be the immediate go-to choice.

Consumers perceive brands with stronger images as superior to others and may not feel the need to evaluate alternatives. For example, when faced with two different smartphones, the one with the stronger and better brand image is far more likely to be chosen.

A strong brand image provides emotional comfort and a sense of validation when making a purchase decision. It also offers social and psychological value to consumers (e.g., identification, prestige, self-expression). For instance, buying a Tesla isn't just about owning a car—it's also purchasing an identity of 'innovation and environmental consciousness.'

Post-purchase satisfaction levels either strengthen or weaken trust in the brand. A strong brand image can tolerate minor setbacks. For example, even if an Apple product has a small technical issue, the consumer often remains satisfied overall due to the brand's strong perception.

The specific effects of brand image on consumer behavior are summarized in the table below.

Table 1. The Spesific effects of brand image on consumer behaviour.

Effect	Explanation
Increases Perceived Quality	Brand image directly influences consumers' perception of the product's quality.
Reduces Purchase Risk	Strong brands reduce uncertainty and doubts in the purchasing decision.
Builds Emotional Connection	Brand image creates an emotional relationship with consumers, increasing loyalty.
Provides Social Identity	The brand gives consumers a sense of identity or prestige within society.
Creates Loyalty and Recommendation Effect	A good brand experience encourages repeat purchases and recommending the brand to others.

Brand image is an invisible yet decisive force that influences consumers throughout all stages of the purchasing process. A strong brand image doesn't just boost sales—it also fosters brand loyalty, word-of-mouth marketing, and long-term customer relationships.

6.3. Brand Loyalty, Trust, and Purchase Intent

In previous sections, we briefly touched on how a positive brand image can increase consumer trust, reinforce loyalty, and boost the likelihood of a product or service being chosen. Numerous studies have shown that a favorable brand image strengthens consumers' perception of quality, reduces price sensitivity, and increases repurchase intent.

The stronger and more positive the brand image, the more consumers' purchasing decisions lean in favor of the brand. Therefore, businesses can strategically manage their brand image to influence consumer behavior and gain a competitive edge. A positive and strong brand image directly affects how consumers perceive the brand.

Consumers evaluate brands they trust and have a positive image of through a different perceptual filter. For example, consumers may approach a new product from a brand with a strong quality image more positively, even perceiving it as high-quality before trying it. Here, brand trust comes into play; since a positive brand image creates pre-existing trust in consumers, new information is processed within this favorable framework.

As a result, brand image becomes a prism for consumer perception: if the consumer "likes" the brand, they may overlook flaws or tolerate negative experiences.(en.wikipedia.org)

Building brand loyalty and, consequently, fostering trust among consumers directly influences purchase intent. Here, it's crucial to craft the brand image strategically. Where we position the brand, the benefits we offer consumers, and the perceptions formed through their experiences are all critical. A positive trajectory in this process fosters an emotional connection between the brand and the consumer, motivating repeat purchases. Of course, nurturing the brand image afterward is equally important. For instance, through corporate social responsibility initiatives, the brand image can evolve into an even stronger one, associated with social awareness.

Another key aspect of brand image management is leveraging consumer feedback and interactions within the brand-consumer cycle to guide repositioning efforts. Brands should not be indifferent to consumer reactions or demands, yet radical changes can also harm the brand image. Therefore, a delicate and balanced approach is essential.

In conclusion, a well-planned and structured brand image fosters trust and loyalty. The trust and loyalty consumers develop toward a brand directly influence their purchasing tendencies. Brands that achieve this will see consumers repeatedly choosing their products due to the positive image they've cultivated—whether it's reliability, trustworthiness, eco-friendliness, health-consciousness, or affordability.

6.4. The Interaction Between Brand Image's Emotional and Functional Dimensions and Consumer Preferences

Numerous studies in academic literature confirm the decisive impact of brand image on consumer behavior. Research has particularly found that businesses with a positive brand image are perceived as more trustworthy and preferable by consumers. A favorable image significantly influences not only purchase intention but also critical variables like customer satisfaction, repeat purchase behavior, and brand loyalty (Aaker, 1996; Keller, 1993). The primary reason for this effect is that brands with positive images, create favorable associations in consumers' minds and hold the potential to build strong emotional bonds over time.

From a consumer psychology perspective, brand preference is not merely a rational decision based on a product's functional attributes or price. On the contrary, consumers often develop emotional attachments to brands, which largely guide their choices. In this context, when consumers identify with a brand, their inclination toward it increases; they may even prefer it over more affordable alternatives of similar products. This occurs because a strong brand image reduces perceived risk, lowers post-purchase regret, and makes consumers feel they've made the "right decision."

On the other hand, a negative or weak brand image can pose a significant barrier in the purchasing process. Consumers often perceive brands with poor images as unreliable, low-quality, or unsuitable options, excluding them from their consideration sets. This effect is particularly pronounced in high-involvement product categories (e.g., technology, automobiles, or cosmetics).

Brands should not limit themselves to offering functional utility to consumers; they must also create emotional value. Today's consumers care not only about product performance but also about the values a brand represents, its symbolic meanings, and the relationship it builds with them. Consequently, brands that engage consumers on an emotional level develop stronger loyalty bonds and sustain long-term brand commitment (Schmitt, 1999).

In this context, a reciprocal cycle emerges between brand image and consumer preference. As consumers develop a positive image of a brand, their affinity for it grows, leading to increased interaction, which further reinforces their brand experiences. Similarly, when a brand consistently maintains its experiential offerings and communication tone to preserve this positive image, it fosters enduring consumer trust—the foundation of brand loyalty.

However, when consumer experience contradicts brand image, the emotional bond can be severely damaged. For instance, if there's a disconnect between the values promised in a brand's marketing and its actual product performance, consumers experience disappointment, tarnishing the brand image. Thus, businesses must not only focus on building a strong brand image but also make strategic efforts to align it with consumer experience and ensure its continuity.

In conclusion, brand image has a significant impact on consumer preference through both its emotional and functional dimensions. Brand image should be regarded as an indispensable element in delivering value to consumers, fostering loyalty, creating psychological trust, and ultimately gaining a competitive edge. Therefore, for brands to build a strong perception—both sensory and rational—is key to long-term brand success.

6.5. The Relationship Between Brand Image and Consumer Experience

One way to understand the interaction between brand image, consumer perception, and purchasing behavior is to model it through the communication process. Brand messages delivered by the company (e.g., the brand story in advertising, product packaging design, store atmosphere) are presented as inputs to the consumer's perceptual system. The consumer filters these inputs through their own lens, forming a perception of the brand. If this perception is positive, the consumer develops a favorable attitude toward the brand, makes a purchase, and remains satisfied. In this case, they share their experiences and emotions with others, effectively providing feedback to the brand's image (e.g., through recommendations or social media comments).

These feedbacks spread to wider audiences, influencing other consumers' perceptions of the brand and thereby reinforcing or altering the brand's overall image. In other words, each consumer experience adds a piece to the brand's reputation mosaic. This cycle highlights the importance of consistency and consumer-centricity in brand management. The brand's message must align with the consumer's experience for perception management to succeed and the desired image to be sustained.

On the other hand, consumer perceptions shape and transform brand image over time. Consumers' experiences with a brand, the comments they hear, and their observations alter their perceptions, and these collective shifts in perception form the brand's overall image. For example, if a brand faces repeated quality issues that negatively impact consumer perceptions, over time, the brand's market-wide image may begin to be labeled as 'low-quality.' In this case, perception management has fallen short, and the brand image has been shaped by unfavorable consumer perceptions.

In summary, the interaction between brand image and consumer perception can be viewed as a causality loop. A strong brand image creates positive consumer perceptions, and positive consumer perceptions, in turn, reinforce the brand's image. Sustaining this positive cycle is one of the core objectives of brand management. Otherwise, a negative vicious cycle may emerge: a poor image breeds unfavorable perceptions, which further degrade the image. In the following sections, case studies from various industries will illustrate this interaction in concrete terms.

CHAPTER 7
SECTORAL AND CATEGORICAL ANALYSES

In this section, examples are emphasized to help concretely visualize the academically and technically examined topics in our minds. The examples we present from different sectors will more clearly demonstrate the link and relationship between brand image and purchasing behavior.

7.1. Brand Image and Purchasing Behavior in the Food and Beverage Industry

In the food and beverage industry, brand image is directly linked to product safety, hygiene perception, and taste expectations. Consumers tend to favor 'familiar' and 'trustworthy' brands in this sector (Schiffman & Wisenblit, 2019). Brands like Ülker, Coca-Cola, and Nestlé have become synonymous with tradition, quality, and flavor in consumers' minds. Packaging design, advertising language, and brand history, in particular, are powerful image elements that shape purchasing behavior in this industry. As trust in a brand grows, so does consumer brand loyalty.

In the food industry, brand image strongly influences both perceived taste and trust factors for consumers. Especially in the fast-food sector, a brand's image plays a critical role in shaping consumer perception and driving purchase decisions.

For example, McDonald's, one of the world's largest fast-food chains, has long been associated with an image of affordable, quick, and tasty meals. Consumers know exactly what to expect when they see the McDonald's logo: consistent flavor, fast service, and accessibility. This recognizability and consistency have homogenized the brand's perception on a global scale. Indeed, even for a child, the McDonald's logo can make food seem more appealing; the brand's fun and tasty image psychologically influences the product experience. Studies show that children perceive the same food as tastier when presented with a brand logo. This demonstrates the impact of brand image on perceived taste. Because consumers associate the brand with positive cues (e.g., the smell of fries, toy-filled kids' meals, cheerful colors), their tangible product perception is shaped accordingly.

However, in the food industry, brand image isn't limited to taste perception. With the rise of healthy lifestyle trends, the 'unhealthy' image of fast-food brands can negatively affect consumer perception. In the early 2000s, McDonald's and similar chains faced image issues due to high-calorie, low-nutrition menus. Consumers began perceiving these brands as harmful to health, and this perception impacted sales. In response, companies implemented perception management strategies: McDonald's tried to improve its image by adding healthier options like salads and fruit slices to its menu and emphasizing fresh, quality ingredients in campaigns. The goal was to shift consumer perception toward seeing the brand as 'not just tasty but also offering healthier choices.' To some extent, they succeeded, with consumers at least acknowledging these efforts and softening their stance.

In conclusion, the relationship between brand image and consumer perception in the food industry is multidimensional. Numerous factors, from taste perception to health and safety perceptions, play a role in this dynamic. Successful food brands must build an image that not only appeals to consumers' palates but also fosters trust and loyalty. To achieve this, keeping up with shifting consumer trends and effectively managing perception is essential.

7.2.　Consumer Perception in the Fashion and Apparel Industry

In the apparel industry, a brand is not just a product but also an indicator of a "lifestyle." Fashion brands build consumer perception through aesthetics, originality, and social status. Brand perception can be decisive in how individuals express themselves (Kapferer, 2008). Thus, concepts like brand, brand image, consumer-brand relationships, and loyalty hold even greater significance, especially in the fashion and apparel sector. Some brands exhibit such fascinating dynamics that their self-confidence surprises me. For instance, in recent years, Paul & Shark has forged such a strong bond with its consumers that it no longer even needs to use its iconic shark logo on many of its products.

7.2.1. Luxury Brands and Brand Prestige

Luxury brands (e.g., Gucci, Chanel) offer consumers status, exclusivity, and aesthetic value. In this context, brand image represents an identity far beyond price. The perception of prestige creates emotional satisfaction in purchasing decisions (Vigneron & Johnson, 1999). Gestures made by such high-end brands for their consumers on special occasions enhance their sense of worth and deepen brand loyalty.

7.2.2. Fast Fashion and Price Perception

Fast fashion brands like Zara and H&M cultivate an image of "accessible trends" through affordable pricing and frequent collection updates. Here, brand perception is shaped more by the "style-price balance." Consumers in this segment prioritize fashion relevance and price advantages over quality. The value, benefits, and brand positioning these brands offer create a distinct loyal customer base. In an era where life moves rapidly, everything is consumed quickly, and products almost seem to have expiration dates, brands that swiftly respond to consumer expectations and follow trends generate purchase motivation through positive perception—as long as they fully meet those expectations.

7.3. The Role of Brand Image in Technology Products

In technology products, brand image is built on perceptions of high performance, security, and innovation. Particularly with mobile devices and electronics, consumers may make image-based decisions rather than technical evaluations. The most tangible examples are Apple-branded phones and laptops. A majority of consumers tend to purchase directly without detailed consideration of alternatives, largely due to the power of brand image. Of course, achieving this is no easy feat. Strategic brand management and image-building efforts, backed by the right infrastructure, have elevated the brand and its image above the product itself.

7.3.1. Brand Innovation and Perceived Quality

Brands like Apple, Samsung, and Dyson reinforce their image through continuous innovation and perceptions of superior design. Perceived quality enhances brand trust and product value (Keller, 2001). Consumers form deep emotional bonds with these brands, almost becoming fanatics. Thus, a strong brand image solidifies loyalty, trust, and purchase motivation among consumers. Beyond this stage, minor setbacks hardly shake the brand or its image, turning them into easily manageable processes.

7.3.2. Consumer Confidence and Technological Product Purchases

When it comes to high-priced and technical products, consumers tend to favor only well-known and trusted brands due to perceived risks. As a result, a strong brand image simplifies the decision-making process and reinforces consumer confidence. Consumers act by weighing price against quality and will avoid products that fail to meet their expectations, even if the price is low.

7.4. Brand Image and Consumer Loyalty in the Service Sector

In the service sector (banking, tourism, healthcare, etc.), brand image is experience-driven. The quality of service provided, customer relations, and digital experience elements shape this image. A strong service brand fosters loyalty, increases the likelihood of repeat business, and encourages positive word-of-mouth. For example, brands like Turkish Airlines or Garanti BBVA reinforce their brand image by associating customer satisfaction with service quality.

However, negative experiences can also severely damage a brand's image. Remember that consumers sharing negative experiences far outnumber those sharing positive ones. Therefore, satisfaction surveys must be conducted, any issues identified, and efforts made to address customer concerns. Negative perceptions that may arise in customers' minds should be eliminated—communication must be continued to remove it. The aim here is to protect the service of the brand after the negative experience of the consumer and to save the consumer from the feeling of being alone with the problem they are experiencing. Such approaches reinforce the strong brand image in the consumer's mind despite the negativities they experience at the beginning. The troubles experienced at the beginning are forgotten. Of course, these deficiencies should be eliminated and should not happen again. Otherwise, our image-correcting activities will have no meaning.

CHAPTER 8

APPROACHES AND COMPARISON IN NATIONAL AND INTERNATIONAL MEDIA

Here, national, regional and cultural factors are effective in the development of different consumer behaviors. Many criteria such as cultural structure, traditions, education level, development level, purchasing power, young and old population ratios, political structure, technical infrastructure and people's income level affect purchasing tendencies.

Here, the reason why people do not buy your brand or products is not the price of your product, its quality or algorithms. The most important concept here is trust. People don't trust your brand and product enough to buy it. Then it would be perfectly logical to start with building trust. Therefore, first creating the brand, creating an audience, arousing curiosity and then producing will ensure much higher sales performance. From this point of view, comparing national and international literature reviews will ensure that concepts and approaches are settled in our minds.

8.1.   Brand Image Perception and Consumer Behavior in Developed Countries

In developed countries, brand image is not only the product performance of the consumer; it is also shaped based on the symbolic values and corporate stance of the brand (Kapferer, 2008). As we mentioned above, the trust that strengthens the brand image before the product and attracting the attention of a certain audience directly affect sales, regardless of how much price or quality level the product is put on the market.

For example, studies conducted in countries such as the USA, Germany, and Japan show that consumers associate strong brand images with elements such as trust, quality, and sustainability (Keller, 2001). In these markets, consumers act on factors such as past experience, brand loyalty, social status expectations, and environmental awareness.

Brand perception functions as a filter that directs consumer behavior on both rational and emotional levels. In addition, the prevalence of digitalization in developed countries has made the brand image more actively shaped by the consumer (Hollebeek & Chen, 2014). For such a strong perception, the use of digital platforms and social media will enable reaching serious audiences. The use of people with a certain audience as brand faces and the individual characteristics of this person help to determine the perception of the brand and the audiences to be reached.

8.2. Differentiation of Brand Image Perception in Developing Countries

In developing countries, brand image is closely related not only to the perceived quality of a product or service but also to societal status, the desire to modernize, and the willingness to be included in global identity. In these countries, brands have become a symbol of the economic development process and are positioned as status indicators representing the "western lifestyle" in the eyes of consumers (Batra et al., 2000; Özsomer, 2012). In particular, rapid urbanization, increase in income levels and global media influence are reshaping individuals' consumption behaviors and brand perceptions.

Studies conducted in countries such as China, India, Brazil, and Turkey reveal that consumers often associate foreign origin brands with high quality, reliability, and social prestige. In this context, brand image includes not only the functional benefit of the product but also the concepts of social approval and "visible consumption". Especially among middle-class consumers, the use of foreign brands is seen as a symbol of individual success, economic power and modern life.

In Turkey, this situation is clearly observed in sectors such as fashion, technology and automotive. Consumers feel an emotional affinity for domestic brands, positioning foreign brands as superior in terms of quality, durability, and international relevance. This perception can be considered as a reflection of the processes of "westernization" and "global integration". However, in recent years, it is seen that domestic brands have gained strength in the eyes of consumers with their emphasis on national identity and cultural heritage. For example, brands such as Vestel, TOGG or LC Waikiki develop strategies to increase consumer trust through their "domestic but global" image.

Another factor shaping brand image in emerging markets is the cultural adaptation strategies of brands. Communication styles that align with cultural norms, religious values, and social behavior patterns directly impact brand acceptance. Western brands are taking approaches that make sense of local identity in these markets, sometimes creating ads in local languages or incorporating cultural symbols into their campaigns. For instance, McDonald's in India adapting its menu to religious sensitivities or Nike in Turkey implementing campaigns emphasizing the cultural dimension of sports are strategic steps towards rebuilding brand image within the local context.

As a result, brand image in developing countries carries more symbolic meaning compared to developed markets. Rather than emotional connection, the representation of status, prestige and identity comes to the fore. However, this trend varies depending not only on the global identity of brands, but also on the extent to which they respect local values. Therefore, a successful brand image strategy in these countries requires positioning itself at the intersection of global standards and local sensibilities.

8.3. Evaluation of Studies on Brand Image in Turkey

Academic studies on brand image in Turkey have increased rapidly in both marketing literature and consumer behavior research, especially since the 2000s. During this period, the branding process was associated not only with the competitiveness of businesses but also with the positioning of the country's economy in global markets. Turkey's economic growth trend, the expansion of the middle class and the differentiation of consumer culture have deepened the academic interest in the concept of brand image.

Most of the studies in the literature examine the effects of brand image on consumer purchase intention, brand loyalty and perceived quality. These researches, which are mostly conducted with survey-based quantitative methods, show that consumers emphasize rational criteria such as "quality", "trust", "price" and "recognition" in brand selection; however, psychological factors such as "emotional commitment", "brand story" and "identity alignment" have also become important in recent years (Yılmaz & Kara, 2013; Erdem & Şimşek, 2017). Especially among young consumers, brands' social media performance, social sensitivity, and sustainability policies stand out as the new determinants of brand image.

One of the factors that shape the brand image in Turkey is cultural values and family structure. The collectivist characteristics of society increase the influence of the social environment, family members and close friend groups in the purchasing decisions of individuals. Therefore, brands are positioned not only through individual benefit but also through messages of "social acceptance" and "harmony." In the domestic literature, especially in the analyzes based on Hofstede's cultural dimensions approach, it has been revealed that the characteristics of the Turkish consumer such as "avoiding uncertainty" and "seeking belonging" directly affect the perception of brand image (Kırcova & Enginkaya, 2015).

With the acceleration of digitalization in Turkey in recent years, brand image has started to be redefined in online environments. Researchers such as Özdemir and Acar (2020) emphasize that social media platforms increase the level of trust, transparency and interaction in brand-consumer relationships. Campaigns conducted on digital media, consumer feedback, and influencer influence play critical roles in building brands' images. Especially among Generation Z consumers, the online visibility of brands, social responsibility messages and digital experience quality have become the main determinants of brand perception.

In addition, in the last five years, consumer trend research, sector reports and brand indices carried out in cooperation with public institutions, research centers and the private sector have brought brand image studies to a more institutional basis. Turkish Exporters Assembly (TIM), Capital Magazine's "Turkey's Most Admired Companies" research, IPSOS and Deloitte's consumer trend reports provide the opportunity to continuously measure the image management strategies of brands. In this way, brands can now track not only their past performance but also the dynamic image changes in the consumer's mind.

As a result, academic and sectoral studies on brand image in Turkey **have evolved from a traditional marketing approach to an integrated structure covering digital and cultural dimensions. The success criteria of brands are no longer measured only by product quality, but also by digital interaction power, cultural harmony, social responsibility and sustainable brand identity. In this context, Turkish literature is increasingly integrated with global branding**

discussions and offers strategic insights to enhance the international competitiveness of domestic brands.

8.4. The Effect of Cultural Variables on Brand Image and Purchasing Behavior

Culture forms a decisive background in the perception of brand image. According to Hofstede's theory of cultural dimensions, brand image is seen as a means of personal expression in individualistic societies (e.g. USA, UK); In collectivist societies (e.g., Turkey, China), social acceptance and intra-group influence of the brand are more important (Hofstede, 2001). Therefore, the same brand can have different meanings in different cultural environments. For example, while the Levi's brand has the connotation of youth and freedom in the USA; It can be a symbol of modernity and westernness in Middle Eastern countries.

In purchasing behavior, cultural codes directly influence the way symbols are interpreted, shaping a brand's level of success. For this reason, brand strategies that take into account the cultural context are more successful and sustainable. This perception process is highly subjective and individual. Each consumer may perceive the same brand message or product in different ways. For example, while a perfume advertisement may draw an attractive and high-quality image for some, it may seem exaggerated or repulsive to others. This difference; It is affected by cultural and social factors as well as internal factors such as the consumer's past experiences, expectations, needs and current mood (en.wikipedia.org). Marketers try to understand these differences in consumers' perceptions and try to design messages that are as appropriate to the target audience as possible.

Consumer behavior is a discipline that examines the process by which consumers decide to purchase a product or service and the factors that influence this process. In this process, perception plays an important role as one of the psychological determinants of consumer behavior. The perception process covers the stages from the consumer's receiving and processing of sensory information to making sense of it (en.wikipedia.org). The consumer first hears (sensing) the stimuli coming from marketing communications (advertising, packaging, price, etc.), then decides which of them to pay attention to (selective attention) and finally interprets them according to their own experiences and beliefs. (Interpretation)(en.wikipedia.org)

CHAPTER 9
APPROACH SUGGESTIONS TO IMPROVE BRAND IMAGE

Brand image is an integrated reflection of associations, emotions and experiences related to the brand in the mind of the consumer. Therefore, understanding and measuring the brand image is not limited to visual identity or communication elements; it requires a multi-layered structure that includes cognitive, emotional and symbolic dimensions. It guides strategic marketing decisions by revealing its relationships with variables such as the perceived value of the brand, consumer trust, brand loyalty, and purchase intention.

9.1. Brand Image – Purchasing Behavior Relationship

The relationship between brand image and purchasing behavior is closely linked to the functioning of consumer psychology at the cognitive and emotional level. Keller (1993) emphasizes that brand associations, brand awareness and perceived quality are effective in the consumer decision process in the consumer-based brand value model. In the conceptual model developed in this context; The effect of image components such as brand awareness, brand associations, perceived quality, and trust in the brand on purchase intention and purchasing behavior is structured at the theoretical level. This model can be placed on three main axes:

1. **Cognitive Dimension: The** consumer evaluates their knowledge and impressions about the brand. Product quality, technical features and past experiences are shaped in this dimension.

2. **Emotional Dimension (Affective):** The emotional bond established with the brand and the feelings it evokes in the consumer (e.g. trust, nostalgia).

3. **Behavioral Dimension:** Action-based outcomes such as purchase intention, brand loyalty, and repeat purchase behavior.

Studies supporting this model have shown how brand image components drive consumer decision-making, particularly in the technology (Apple, Samsung), food (Ulker, Coca-Cola), and fashion industries (Schiffman & Wisenblit, 2019; Aaker, 1996). Especially in the digital age, this model needs to be constantly reviewed with dynamic structures and social media effects need to be integrated into the model.

9.2. Strategic Implications for Brand Image Management for Businesses

Brand image management should be part of the strategic vision throughout the organization, not just marketing departments. Aaker (1996) argues that brand management can become sustainable through consistency, differentiation, and long-term identity construction. In this context, the key strategic takeaways that can be recommended for businesses are:

1. **Consistent Brand Identity**: Visual, linguistic, and experiential integrity should be ensured across all communication channels. Creating a stable image in the mind of the consumer is the foundation of trust.

2. **Experience Orientation: The** experience provided to the consumer shapes the brand image as well as the product or service. Therefore, the customer journey should be carefully planned.

3. **Data-Driven Brand Monitoring: Brand** image should be constantly monitored with data such as social media analytics, online comments and NPS scores; negativities should be intervened early.

4. **Crisis Communication Competence:** Brand image can be damaged during crisis periods. Therefore,

transparent, fast and effective communication strategies should be in place.

5. **Cultural Adaptation:** Especially for international brands, it is imperative to develop brand strategies that are compatible with the local culture (Hofstede, 2001).

These strategies ensure that the brand image is not only aesthetic; It ensures that it is treated as a strategic capital. Successful brand image management is not only about market share; It also directly affects reputation, loyalty and pricing power.

9.3. Cross-Cultural Comparative Studies

How the perception of brand image is shaped in different cultural structures has not yet been discussed in sufficient depth. Cultural models such as Hofstede (2001) should be used more frequently. Especially in recent years, there has been change in every field in the world and naturally change in cultures is inevitable. Since the studies based on the old generation cultural understanding are generally studies carried out, it may cause some issues to be not fully understood. Therefore, research on different cultures all over the world and their comparisons will provide serious benefits in the development of brands, products, brand images and strategies and in the management of all these processes.

9.4. Digital Brand Image

Social media, influencer influence, and the impact of online user reviews on brand image are still a dynamic area of research. These issues should be deepened with quantitative and qualitative methods. The data obtained after the studies carried out by selecting the pilot regions and subjects will guide the extensive studies to be carried out in the next period.

It should be investigated how consumer interaction with new technologies (e.g., ChatGPT, virtual customer representatives) transforms brand perception. After digitalization, more comprehensive research should be conducted on shopping types, marketing techniques, consumer perceptions and behavior patterns.

9.5. Sectoral Depth

In areas such as food, FMCG, luxury products and the service sector, the brand image-purchasing relationship should be examined in a sectoral context. Working models to be created by taking into account the unique dynamics of each sector can be considered as resources that will shed light on that sector and will be used when developing strategies for brands.

These expansions will both contribute to the theoretical development of marketing science and guide the application strategies of businesses. Especially in the context of Turkey, domestic trademark research compatible with cultural codes will make significant contributions to the literature.

CHAPTER 10

CONCLUSION AND EVALUATION

Brand image has become one of the main determinants of modern consumption behaviors and has been accepted as a strategic value area in both marketing literature and business practices. Theoretical analyses, sectoral evaluations, cultural comparisons and conceptual model proposals made within the scope of this study revealed that the relationship between brand image and consumer behavior has a multidimensional and dynamic structure. The concept of brand image, which is revealed in all its dimensions with this study, will guide brand building, brand management and brand strategy.

In the analyzes made especially in the food, technology, fashion and service sectors, it is seen that brand image components (awareness, association, trust, perceived quality) are decisive on purchasing intention and behavior. In addition, the perception of brand image differs in developed and developing countries; factors such as cultural values, economic level and digitalization are reshaping this perception (Kapferer, 2008; Hofstede, 2001).

Sectoral analyses show that brand image perception differs according to sector dynamics. While the perception of trust and hygiene is at the forefront in the food and beverage industry; Style, status and identity representation are decisive in the fashion industry. Innovation and functionality in technology products, and experience and customer satisfaction in the service sector come to the fore. This differentiation makes it essential for each industry to customize its brand image management strategies.

Within the scope of the research, many strategic implications for businesses were put forward in terms of application:

1. Brand image management should be a part of a holistic corporate communication strategy, not just marketing.

2. In the digital age, online brand experience, user reviews, and social media interactions are at least as influential determinants of brand image as traditional advertising.

3. In brand crises, transparent communication and trust-based strategies are key to maintaining image.

As a result, the conceptual approach and practical examples show that businesses should position brand building not only as a symbolic tool but also as a strategic competitive element. The relationship between brand image and consumer behavior is multidimensional and dynamic. In this context, various research areas are proposed for future studies in order to contribute to the accumulation in the literature and to develop theoretical approaches practically. These proposals aim to offer new expansions both theoretically and sectorally:

Brand image is directly affected by the cultural value system of the consumer. For this reason, research that comparatively examines how the same brand is perceived in societies with different cultural codes is important. For example, the emphasis on individuality in Western societies and collectivism-based approaches in Asian cultures can lead to different consumer reactions to the same brand image. In this context, cross-cultural empirical studies can also guide the localization of universal brand strategies.

The digitalized consumer experience has caused brand perception to move from the physical environment to the virtual environment. In this process, elements such as digital interfaces, web design, mobile application experience and social media representation have become the new determinants of brand image. Therefore, studies comparing the brand image on digital platforms with the image in the physical store environment are of great importance in terms of both academic and applied marketing.

In the literature, the relationship between brand image and general consumer behavior has been examined mostly in B2C sectors. However, in B2B markets, the function of brand image is also important in less researched areas such as healthcare, education, utilities, and financial services. Since the decision processes in these sectors are more complex, perception management should be handled in more strategic dimensions. Research focusing on such areas has the potential to expand brand image theories.

The Impact of Artificial Intelligence and Algorithmic Marketing makes him feel extremely strong in this regard. Today, chatbots, recommendation engines, automated content management systems, and personalized advertising algorithms are changing the nature of interaction between consumers and brands. How these technologies create an image in consumer perception, how they affect the level of trust and how they can be associated with brand loyalty are still not sufficiently researched. Interdisciplinary studies in this field (marketing, artificial intelligence, behavioral economics) may pave the way for the development of new theoretical models.

It has a very serious contribution to the formation and development of the brand image in Digital Communities and Social Interaction. The brand image formed through influencers, online user reviews, social media campaigns and digital communities has become very effective today. Issues such as how these factors create a relationship of trust, how they establish an emotional bond with the consumer, and how they develop loyalty to the brand, especially among younger generations (Z and Alpha), have a rich potential for future research. In particular, experimental studies are needed to examine the effect of social media together with neuropsychological reactions.

Sustainability-Based Brand Perception!

What kind of image brands that are environmentally friendly, ethical or support social responsibility projects create in the eyes of consumers is a rising research area in today's literature. Questions such as to what extent consumers' perception of a "green brand" or "ethical brand" coincides with their purchasing tendencies and how it changes in different income and cultural groups will provide important data in guiding sustainable brand strategies.

Change in Brand Image Perception with Time Series!

Brand image is not a fixed perception but a perception that changes over time. Long-term studies based on time series analyses, which examine how consumer perception evolves, especially after brand crises, negative news, scandals or brand transformation campaigns, are very valuable. Such studies can make practical contributions to image reconstruction, post-crisis recovery, and strategic communication management.

These suggestions aim to provide new theoretical contributions in terms of academic knowledge production and to enable practitioners to make more effective decisions in marketing strategies. Considering that the phenomenon of brand image should be understood not only as a communicative tool but also as a complex structure that directs consumer behavior, designing future studies in a way that includes interdisciplinary, empirical and sectoral diversity will provide more detailed and concrete results.

The findings of this study have allowed the relationship between brand image and consumer behavior to be discussed from different perspectives and have made both theoretical and practical contributions to the existing literature. However, considering some limitations of the research, it is understood that the results should be supported by more comprehensive studies that will be handled with different orientations.

Finally, the expansion of research in international and cross-cultural contexts will shed light on how brand image and consumer behavior are shaped under different cultural, socioeconomic, and geographical conditions. Such studies will both provide a global perspective to the academic literature and contribute to shaping the international branding strategies of businesses.

REFERENCES

Aaker, D. A. (1996).*Building Strong Brands*. New York: Free Press.

AutoPacific Survey (2015).*Volkswagen Trust Aftermath*.

https://en.wikipedia.org

Hofstede, G. (2001).*Culture's consequences: Comparing values, behaviors, institutions and organizations across nations*(2. Edition). Thousand Oaks, CA: Sage Publications.

Hollebeek, L. D., & Chen, T. (2014). Exploring customer brand engagement: Definition and Themes.*Journal of Strategic Marketing, 22*(7), 555–573.

https://doi.org/10.1080/0965254X.2014.914063

Kapferer, J. N. (2008).*The new strategic brand management: Creating and sustaining brand equity long term*(4. Edition). London: Kogan Page Publishers.

Keller, K. L. (1993).Conceptualizing, measuring, and managing customer-based brand equity. *Journal of Marketing, 57*(1), 1-22.

Keller, K. L. (2001). Building customer-based brand equity: A blueprint for creating strong brands. *Marketing Management, 10*(2), 15–19.

Kotler, P., & Keller, K. L. (2016).*Marketing management* (15. Edition). Pearson Education.

Özdemir, S., & Acar, A. (2020). A study on digital brand perception and e-commerce experience in Turkey.*Journal of Marketing Theory and Practices*, *6*(1), 1–15.

Plumeyer, A., Kottemann, P., Böger, D., & Decker, R. (2019). Measuring brand image: a systematic review, practical guidance, and future research directions.*Review of Managerial Science*, *13*(2), 227–265.

Reuters. (2015).*VW scandal threatens 'Made in Germany' brand.* https://en.wikipedia.org

Schiffman, L. G., & Wisenblit, J. (2019).*Consumer behavior*(12. Edition). New York: Pearson.

Schmitt, B. (1999). Experiential marketing.*Journal of Marketing Management*, *15*(1–3), 53–67.

https://doi.org/10.1362/026725799784870496

Vigneron, F., & Johnson, L. W. (1999). A review and a conceptual framework of prestige-seeking consumer behavior.*Academy of Marketing Science Review*, *1999*(1), 1–15.

Perception management. (n.d.).*Wikipedia.*https://tr.wikipedia.org

Brand. (n.d.)., *Wikipedia.*https://tr.wikipedia.org

Consumer Behaviour. (n.d.). *Wikipedia.* https://tr.wikipedia.org

Volkswagen emissions scandal.

(n.d.). *Wikipedia.* https://tr.wikipedia.org

Yılmaz, C., & Kara, A. (2013). A study on the relationship between consumers' brand loyalty and perceived brand image. *Anadolu University Journal of Social Sciences, 13*(2), 45–60.

PART 2

BRAND STRATEGIES AND TRANSFORMATION OF BRAND IMAGE IN THE DIGITAL WORLD

CHAPTER 1
WHAT IS BRAND IMAGE TRANSFORMATION AND BRAND MANAGEMENT IN THE DIGITAL WORLD?

1. INTRODUCTION

Digitalization is not only a technological renewal process, but has also become a paradigm that radically changes the dynamics of the entire business world with its economic, cultural and managerial dimensions. This transformation redefines the relationships brands establish with consumers, brand positioning strategies, communication styles, and value creation processes. One-way communication models, which are the basis of traditional marketing approaches, have now been replaced by two-way, interaction-based and participatory brand-consumer relations. In this context, the digitalization process has enabled brands to become entities that build meaning, experience, and community within digital ecosystems, rather than just institutions offering products or services.

Branding in the digital environment requires new skills at both a strategic and operational level. Brands now have to display a consistent image across different platforms with omnichannel communication strategies, manage consumer interactions, and optimize decision-making processes with real-time data analysis. In this context, digital transformation is not just an element of competitive advantage; It has become a basic strategic necessity that determines the sustainability of brands. Especially social media, e-commerce platforms, mobile applications and digital communities play a critical role in building the identity of brands.

In this section, the main purpose of addressing the issue of brand strategies and **brand image transformation in the digital world is to examine the reconstruction of brand strategies by taking into account the transformations brought by the digital age**; to analyze the tools of brand management in the digital environment, its application areas and how the brand image is shaped at the theoretical and sectoral level. The study compares traditional brand management approaches in the literature with the innovations offered by the digital ecosystem; It aims to discuss how basic concepts such as "brand perception", "consumer trust", "loyalty" and "brand experience" are redefined in the digital context. In this process, it will be emphasized that digitalization transforms not only marketing strategies, but **also the psychological, sociological and cultural dimensions of the brand-consumer relationship.**

In this context, the main questions of the research are structured as follows:

- How has digitalization affected brand strategies?
- How is the brand image built and sustained in the digital environment?
- How are consumer behaviors affected by digital brand management processes?
- How have traditional brand strategies become reinterpretable in the digital environment?

While seeking answers to these questions, the study will present a holistic evaluation through both theoretical literature review and sectoral case studies. Methodically, the research is structured on three basic axes:

1. **Conceptual Analysis:** Definitions, models and interaction points of digitalization, brand image, consumer behavior and digital brand management concepts in the literature will be examined.

2. **Sectoral Case Studies:** The effects of brands' digital strategies on image, loyalty and awareness will be analyzed with selected examples from Turkish and global markets.

3. **Content-Based Evaluations:** Brands' communication language, use of visual identity and consumer interaction

styles on digital platforms will be evaluated by content analysis method.

This approach aims to highlight brands' ability to establish meaningful and sustainable relationships with consumers, going beyond mere efforts to gain visibility in the age of digitalization. Thus, the study will create a theoretical framework that will both contribute to the academic literature and offer strategic suggestions for digital brand management practices.

CHAPTER 2

CONCEPTUAL FRAMEWORK OF BRAND MANAGEMENT IN THE DIGITAL WORLD

A brand is not just the name or visual representation of a product, but the whole of the perceptions, associations and emotional bonds formed in the consumer's mind. In this context, brand strategy is a set of plans created to manage these perceptions and provide a sustainable competitive advantage in the market.

Brand management has functions such as ensuring the continuity of the relationship established with the target audience, increasing the value of the brand and reinforcing consumer loyalty from the positioning of the brand. In this process, brand image refers to the sum of the impressions that the consumer creates about the brand in their minds. Image can often have a stronger impact than the brand itself and can influence consumer decisions at a decisive level.

In brand value models developed by researchers such as Aaker (1991) and Keller (1993), it is emphasized that factors such as brand awareness, perceived quality, associations and loyalty have strong ties with brand image. Digitalization is not only technical; it also transforms at the semantic level.

For example, in the digital environment, a brand's presence on social media, interaction level, user reviews, and digital PR strategies play a central role in the formation of brand image. For this reason, it is essential for brands to develop digital strategies not only to gain competitive advantage but also to effectively carry out perception management.

In the conceptual framework, the differences between brand management approaches before and after digitalization are also mentioned. While one-way communication is dominant in the traditional model, a versatile, interactive and data-based structure comes to the fore in the digital age. This makes it necessary to personalize brand strategies, segment-based communication, and create brand personality specific to digital platforms.

2.1 The Digitalization Process and the Evolution of the Brand Management Paradigm

Digitalization is not only a technological change but also a socio-economic phenomenon that radically transforms the reason for existence and management of brands. In the traditional period, brands competed within the framework of a product-centered approach; The digital age has transformed brands into experience-centered, data governance-driven organisms.

Aaker (1991) defined the brand as a "value-creating identity system"; Keller (1993), on the other hand, argued that the mental associations of the consumer determine brand power with the Customer-Based Brand Equity (CBBE) model. Today, these theories are being reinterpreted with data analytics, behavioral insight, and interaction economics.

The digitalization process has restructured brand management in four dimensions:

1. **Data-Driven Strategy:** Social media listening, CRM, and big data tools offer real-time monitoring of consumer behavior.

2. **Micro-Segmentation:** Algorithmic models enable understanding of target audiences at the level of micro-communities, rather than being a one-size-fits-all audience.

3. **Interactional Communication:** Brands no longer just convey messages; they produce shared content with the user.

4. **Continuous Learning Brand:** Digitalization transforms the brand into an adaptive learning system (Kapferer, 2012).

Christodoulides (2009) called this transformation the "digital brand management paradigm" and emphasized that brands have become social organisms that not only communicate but **also produce meaning.**

Table 2 – Elements of Digital Brand Management

Size	Description	Strategic Conclusion
Data Management	Analyzing digital data	Targeted marketing, personalization
Content Production	Content that expresses brand equity	Awareness, trust
Omni-Channel Communication	Multi-channel and consistent experience	Loyalty, commitment
Brand Personality	Language, tone, humor, and responsibility	Perceptual difference
Ethical Management	Transparency and sustainability	Reputation and trust

2.2 Digital Reconstruction of Brand Image

Brand image is a holistic perception system of the consumer about a brand, consisting of cognitive (mental evaluations, perceived quality, associations) and emotional (such as trust, belonging, sympathy) elements. However, in the digital age, this image is no longer a static, one-way structure; It has turned into a dynamic organism that reproduces itself in a continuous cycle of interaction, sharing and feedback.

Social media comments, user experiences, influencer posts, and even content recommended by algorithms redefine the brand's image at any time. For this reason, brand image is no longer a perception controlled only by the business, but **a living process shaped by the joint production of consumer communities.**

In other words, in the digital environment, brand image behaves just like an "ecosystem": it changes, adapts, and transforms based on content, engagement, and emotional engagement. This transformation necessitates brands to evolve with the consumer while maintaining their identity.

Digital channels have created 3 basic axes on the brand image:
The digitalization process has led to a radical paradigm shift in the way brand image is formed and managed. Today, brands exist not only with their own corporate communications, but also with an image shaped by the sum of interactions in the digital ecosystem. In this context, digital channels have formed three main axes in the construction of brand image: social media interaction, User-Generated Content (UGC) **and digital opinion leaders (influencers).**

1. Social Media Engagement

Social media is the most powerful communication channel that makes it possible to interact directly in the brand-consumer relationship. The language used by brands, the way they manage their crisis, their responses to followers, and even their choice of silence play a critical role in shaping the brand image. Communication on these platforms is not just about sharing information; It is also considered as an indicator of trust, sincerity and sensitivity. For example, brands that adopt a fast, transparent and empathetic communication style in times of crisis strengthen their reputation in the eyes of consumers; Brands that exhibit a delayed or defensive attitude may experience a loss of image. In addition, social media analytics allows brands to measure consumer perception in real time and update their strategies dynamically. In this way, brands have turned into actors who not only convey messages but also listen and learn from their community.

2. User-Generated Content (UGC)

In today's digital environment, the identity of brands is largely shaped by user-generated content (comments, reviews, unboxing videos, experience sharing, etc.). This type of content is perceived as "authentic" and "reliable" sources of information beyond traditional advertising. Research reveals that consumers rely highly on other user experiences when making purchasing decisions (Cheong & Morrison, 2008). UGC creates both opportunities and risks for brands: positive content organically reinforces the brand image, while negative reviews can spread quickly and undermine the brand's credibility. For this reason, successful brands develop community management strategies by interacting with user content instead of controlling it, and adopt a communication language that embraces the user experience. This approach moves the brand from a "communication authority" to a "digital community leader."

3. Digital Opinion Leaders (Influencers)

Digital opinion leaders are one of the most effective intermediary actors that shape the social perception of brands. As Iglesias and Ind (2016) point out, brand reputation today is built not only through professional advertising campaigns, but also through the personal credibility of opinion leaders and community influence. By integrating the brand with their lifestyle, values, and authentic narratives, influencers create a relationship of trust that goes far beyond traditional media influence. This is especially evident in the younger generation of consumers; Gen Z individuals tend to trust the people who represent the brand, not the brands. For this reason, brands are now developing "value alignment" strategies, not just "influencer collaboration". While the image is strengthened when the ethical values, sustainability policies and social sensitivity of the brand coincide with the identity of the opinion leader; On the contrary, crises of confidence arise.

In conclusion, digital channels represent a shift from a one-way narrative to a multifaceted interactive structure in brand image management. Brands no longer only have to tell their own stories, but also be a part of the stories produced by consumers. These three axes — social media engagement, user-generated content, and digital opinion leaders — demonstrate the dynamic, interactive, and community-based nature of modern brand image; it's redefining both the opportunities and vulnerabilities of brand management in the digital age.

Elements such as brand awareness, associations, perceived quality, and loyalty in Keller's (1993, 2001) CBBE model have gained a new meaning in the digital context. For example, training videos shared by a brand on YouTube reinforce perceived quality, while crisis management on Twitter/X reinforces brand associations.

Kotler et al. (2017) described this process as **"Interactional Brand Equity"**; emphasized that brands should maintain their digital identity consistency through continuous dialogue with the consumer.

2.3. Digital Brand Experience and Redefining Emotional Value

The concept of "experience economy" **put forward by Pine and Gilmore (1999)** has gained a new meaning for brands in today's digital age. Now, consumers value not only the physical benefit of a product or service, but also the emotional connection they establish with the brand, identity harmony and interactive experience. Therefore, digitalization is not just a communication or sales channel for brands; It has become an experience area where meaningful, continuous and multidimensional relationships are established with the consumer.

Schmitt (1999) defines brand experience with emotional (feel**), cognitive (think), behavioral (act)** and relational (relate) components. Digitalization has further deepened these components, transforming the experience into **a holistic life cycle that extends not only to the consumption process but also to the before and after. For example, artificial intelligence-supported personalized recommendations (Spotify, Netflix) strengthen the behavioral component; the value-oriented discourses of the brand (Patagonia, Ben & Jerry's) deepen the relational dimension.** Lemon and Verhoef (2016) identify three key factors for a digital brand experience to be sustainable:

1. **Personalization: The** data collected on digital platforms makes it possible for brands to appeal to consumers on an individual level. This facilitates not only recommendation algorithms but also emotional connection. Personalized email, dynamic web interfaces, location-based campaigns, and recommendations based on past experiences make the consumer feel like a part of the brand. For example, Spotify's "Your Wrapped" feature creates both belonging and emotional sharing by offering user-specific content.

2. **Consistency: The credibility** of the digital brand experience depends on the brand maintaining the same values, tone, and visual language across all digital touchpoints (website, social media, mobile app, e-commerce platform, etc.). Consistency is the foundation of

trust; Because in the digital environment, the consumer constantly observes the behavior of the brand. Apple's minimalist design language or IKEA's simple and simple approach to user experience are examples that reinforce the identity integrity of the brand.

3. **Participation:** The digital experience is no longer just a brand-driven process; it has evolved into a structure where the consumer actively participates in the brand's story. User reviews, social media interactions, online communities, and gamification strategies strengthen consumer identification with the brand. For example, the LEGO Ideas platform is a model that encourages users' participation in the brand's production process by sharing their own designs. Such practices increase not only interaction but **also emotional ownership.**

As a result of this transformation, the digital brand experience **goes beyond classical customer satisfaction and creates a deep emotional attachment**. Today's consumer sees the brand not only as a supplier, but also as a reflection of their own value world. Apple's simple yet prestigious aesthetic, Nike's social sensitivity and motivation-themed campaigns, Starbucks' personalized mobile app experience, or Tesla's emphasis on innovation and sustainability are pioneering examples of this new era.

The digital brand experience has also brought about the **"redefinition of emotional value"**. In the past, trust in brands was shaped by product performance and advertising power, but today, it is based on values such as data privacy, ethical responsibility, environmental awareness and social participation. The consumer expects not only a product but also a stance from the brand. For this reason, brand experience in the digital age can be defined as the process of meaning and identity production rather than functionality.

In conclusion, the digital brand experience is positioned at the intersection of technological innovations and emotional connection strategies. For brands, this is not just the process of creating a digital presence, but strengthening the emotional capital of the brand by establishing continuous and empathetic communication with the consumer. This new approach transforms brands from mere consumption objects into cultural actors of the digital age.

2.4. Brand Management Approaches Before and After Digitalization

Brand management has undergone a radical transformation over the past two decades, driven by technological advancements, changing consumer expectations, and global competitive conditions. Digitalization is not only the way brands communicate; It has also redefined the methods of strategic planning, performance measurement and establishing relationships with the consumer. In the traditional period, brands mainly created perceptions through corporate identity, advertising power and product quality, while in the digital era, interaction, experience and meaning production have become the main strategic axes. The table below illustrates the key differences between traditional brand management and digital brand management:

Table 3. Comparison of brand approaches before and after digitalization

Size	Traditional Brand Management	Digital Brand Management
Contact Now	One-way message transfer; It is based on mass media such as advertising and the press.	Bidirectional, interactive communication; It is carried out through social media, blogs, digital communities.
Source of Information	Sales data, consumer surveys, and market research.	Real-time big data, social media analytics, and artificial intelligence-based behavioral insights.

Brand Personality	Corporate, static, predefined.	Dynamic, community-based, constantly updated.
Strategic Focus	Advertising, promotion and product-oriented marketing.	Experience management, storytelling, and content marketing.
Measurement	Awareness rate, sales volume, market share.	Level of engagement, digital loyalty, emotional value, online trust.
Success Criteria	Market share and brand awareness.	Digital community size, brand reputation, user loyalty.

2.4.1. Effects of Digital Transformation on Brand Management

These differences show that brands are no longer just providers of products and services, **but creators of meaning, experience and community. In the digital age, brands have ceased to be actors that manage communication and have turned into organisms that exist in simultaneous interaction with the consumer. The consumer is no longer a passive buyer, but a "co-creator" who actively shapes the identity and image of the brand** (Prahalad & Ramaswamy, 2004).

While traditional brand management is predominantly based on control and one-way message transfer; Digital brand management is built on the principles of participation, experience and transparency. This situation has created two fundamental transformations in the management approach of brands:

1. **Transition from Authority to Participation:** In the past, brands told consumers "what to think", but today, consumers tell the brand "what will happen". The digital age has shifted the brand discourse from the center to the periphery; social media users, community managers and digital opinion leaders have become the brand's new communication tool.

2. **Transition from Performance to Understanding:** In the traditional understanding, brand success is determined by measurements such as sales volume and market share; In the digital age, brands **are evaluated through their capacity to produce meaning, the emotional bond they establish with the consumer, and value-based communication. The consumer no longer invests in "what he buys", but in "what he believes".**

2.4.2. Strategic Results

This transformation has led brand managers to a more data-driven, agile and story-driven structure. Successful brands no longer create value with "one right message", but **with a consistent identity and personalized experiences across multiple platforms.**

Brands like Nike, Apple, and Tesla are not just technological; it also shows that there is a cultural rebirth.

In conclusion, the main difference between the pre-digitalization era and today's brand management is in the ownership of the "brand narrative":

- In the past, brands used to tell their own stories,
- Today, they write this story together with consumers.

This situation has transformed brand management from just a marketing process into a multi-layered strategic field that includes social interaction, identity construction and meaning production.

2.5. Ethical Brand Management and Sustainability in the Digital Age

While digitalization has created unlimited visibility, accessibility, and interaction opportunities for brands, it has also expanded the scope of ethical responsibilities. Brands are now judged and judged not only by product quality, but also by their digital behavior, data management policies, and social sensitivity levels. In this new era, ethical brand management is not only economical for brands; It has become a part of their social, environmental and cultural performance.

2.5.1. Digital Ethics and Corporate Responsibility

In the digital age, the ethical responsibility areas of brands have expanded on three basic axes:

- Data privacy and algorithmic transparency,
- Social responsibility and environmental sustainability,
- Digital behavioral ethics and representation justice.

Consumers have become more conscious and sensitive about how brands collect, process, and share personal data. Regulations such as the European Union's General Data Protection Regulation (GDPR) have mandated brands to develop ethical data management policies. Now, a "privacy policy" is not just a legal requirement, it's a core component of brand trust. The digital consumer quickly reacts negatively to brands whose personal data is not managed transparently and fairly.

2.5.2. Sustainability and Digital Brand Strategies

Leonidou and Hultman (2011) define digital sustainability strategies as the way businesses strike the balance between economic success and social benefit. According to this perspective, sustainable brand management should include not only environmental awareness but also the principles of fair production, inclusive communication and social equality in the digital ecosystem.

However, the phenomenon of "greenwashing" **emphasized by Parguel et al. (2011)** is one of the biggest ethical risks of the digital age. In the age of social media, the eco-friendly rhetoric of brands is easily verifiable, exposing false sustainability claims in a short time. The digital consumer is no longer a passive buyer, but an actor who researches, questions and controls the brand's behavior through digital footprints. For this reason, brands must not only present an environmentally friendly image, but **also create measurable and verifiable sustainability commitments.**

2.5.3. Basic Dimensions of Ethical Brand Management

Keller and Swaminathan (2020) define ethical brand management in the digital age under three key dimensions:

1. **Transparency:** The purpose, scope and usage patterns of the data collected by brands must be clearly disclosed. Transparency not only creates trust but also holds the brand accountable. Apple, for instance, has strengthened user trust by positioning data privacy as one of its core values.

2. **Consistency: In** the digital landscape, the alignment between brand discourse and actions is a key indicator of ethical trustworthiness. Brands that claim sustainability or social sensitivity quickly lose trust when they do not implement concrete practices to support this discourse. Patagonia's "Don't Buy This Jacket" campaign is a powerful example of the brand's consistency in turning ethical values into action.

3. **Social Contribution:** Ethical brand management requires taking responsibility not only on an individual level but also on a societal level. Showing the sensitivity of brands to social problems on digital platforms is one of the new criteria of reputation. Nike's anti-racist "For Once, Don't Do It" campaign or Unilever's gender equality projects are examples that combine social sensitivity with ethical leadership in the digital age.

2.5.4. Digital Trust and Credibility

In this context, the success of digital brand strategies is no longer measured only by visibility or access rates, but also **by credibility, trust and responsibility perception. The digital reputation of the brand is directly related to how faithful the consumer is to the values they trust. The concept of "ethical alignment" refers to the consistency between the brand's promise and**

societal expectations. When this harmony is disrupted in the digital age, crises can spread within seconds and the image that brands have built for many years can be seriously damaged.

In the digital age, ethical brand management has become not just a moral responsibility but **a strategic imperative. Consumers lead the rise of conscious consumption by choosing brands that are sensitive to the environment, society and the individual. In this context, sustainability has become an integrated value due to the existence of brands; ethical behavior has been the most important capital of brand image.**

2.5.5. Case Studies on Digital Ethics Violations and Brand Crises

One of the most distinctive features of the digital age is the speed at which information flows. This creates both opportunity and risk for brands: just as an innovation can gain global attention in minutes, an ethical violation can quickly turn into a global crisis. Below are some case studies that demonstrate the impact of digital ethical vulnerabilities on brand image.

1. Cambridge Analytica – Facebook Data Privacy Scandal (2018)

In the Cambridge Analytica case, the personal data of millions of users was used to target political ads without their consent. The inadequacy of Facebook's data security policies has led not only to legal investigations but also to serious damage to brand trust. This crisis has shown that digital ethical violations cannot be "invisible" and that transparent data management is of strategic importance for brand reputation.

2. Volkswagen – Emissions Manipulation (2015)

When it was revealed that Volkswagen had manipulated vehicle emission tests, the brand experienced not only financial damage but also a crisis of confidence that would last for many years. The discrepancy between the company's "green technology" rhetoric and its actual practices was quickly exposed by the consumer of the digital age. This example **has clearly demonstrated that the concept of "greenwashing"** is unsustainable in the face of digital monitoring mechanisms.

3. H&M – Critiques of Sustainability and Cultural Sensitivity (2020)

Criticisms that H&M's sustainability claims in the "Conscious" collection do not reflect the truth have had a great impact on social media. Additionally, some of the brand's advertising campaigns have led to calls for boycotts due to cultural insensitivity. These reactions, which spread across digital platforms, led to an erosion of trust in the brand's global image. The case has shown that digital ethics management should include not only environmental but also cultural sensitivity.

4. Uber – Employee Rights and Data Ethics Debate (2017–2021)

Criticism that Uber's algorithmic compensation systems for drivers are unfair, and that user and driver data are not adequately protected, has undermined the brand's digital credibility. This example has clearly shown that ethical management in platform economies requires responsibility not only towards the user but also towards all stakeholders in the ecosystem.

5. Balenciaga – Digital Campaign Crisis (2022)

The images used in the children-themed digital campaign of the luxury fashion brand Balenciaga created inappropriate associations, which started a great wave of reactions on social media. The late and inadequate response of the brand was effective in the growth of the crisis; The incident emphasized that ethical control in the digital age should be carried out in a multi-layered manner not only at the stage of content production but also before publication.

2.5.6. Evaluation

These cases clearly demonstrate the fragility of brand reputation in the digital age. Each example shows that brands need to reconsider not only their communication strategies, but also their data management, cultural representation, social sensitivity and crisis response processes. Digital ethics is no longer just the responsibility of the public relations department, but a management culture that must be adopted throughout the organization.

Brands that embrace the principles of ethical leadership and digital responsibility also have the potential to turn crises into opportunities. For example, Apple's placement of data privacy policies at the center of its advertising campaigns or Patagonia's "don't buy this jacket" approach show that digital trust can be restored.

2.6. Case Studies: Experiences on Digital Brand Activities

This section examines selected case studies to illustrate how digital brand activities are designed, implemented, and managed across different organizational contexts. By focusing on real-world applications, the analysis moves beyond theoretical frameworks to evaluate how digital tools, platforms, and strategies contribute to brand positioning, consumer engagement, and long-term brand equity. The case studies highlight both successful practices and strategic missteps, offering comparative insights into decision-making processes, performance outcomes, and adaptive capabilities in digitally driven brand environments. Through these examples, the section aims to demonstrate how digital brand activities function as dynamic, data-informed, and strategically integrated components of contemporary brand management.

1. Tesla: Branding of Innovation

Tesla is at the forefront of innovation-driven redefinition of digital branding. The corporate identity integrated with Elon Musk's personal brand has given the brand a visionary and revolutionary personality. Tesla's visibility on social media, with almost zero traditional advertising investment, demonstrates the power of the digital age's "community-based communication" model. Consumers are drawn to Tesla's brand not only for its product performance, but also for its belief in the future. This situation reveals that the brand image in the digital age is fed by "innovative vision" instead of "rational value". (Source: Mangram, 2012; Labrecque et al., 2013)

2. Nike: Digital Activism and Social Involvement

In the 2010s, Nike strengthened the brand's social responsibility aspect by combining the "Just Do It" rhetoric with its digital activism strategy. The Colin Kaepernick campaign, in particular, positioned the brand as an "advocate for social justice"; It has created great interaction on social media. This strategy embodied Hollebeek and Chen (2014)'s "consumer engagement" theory; The brand has made its consumers not only a target audience but also a value partner. (Source: Parguel et al., 2011; Holt, 2016)

3. Starbucks: Digital Loyalty and Experiential Engagement

Starbucks is one of the pioneers of digital loyalty with personalized offers and points systems through the mobile application. It uses consumer data not only for marketing purposes, but also to create depth of relationship. In this way, customers who establish an emotional bond with the brand maintain their loyalty despite price changes.

In the brand experience scale defined by Brakus et al. (2009), Starbucks is one of the global brands with the highest scores in the "relate" dimension, that is, in the capacity to establish relationships. (Source: Brakus et al., 2009; Lemon & Verhoef, 2016)

4. Patagonia: Sustainability and Ethical Image

Patagonia has turned its environmental awareness into a central strategy not only in communication but also in its business model. The "Don't Buy This Jacket" campaign in 2011 turned the classical advertising concept on its head with its anti-consumerist message. This discourse has had a wide repercussion on digital platforms; It has increased the credibility of the brand. The Patagonia example shows that ethical behavior can be the brand's strongest image capital in the digital age. (Source: Leonidou & Hultman, 2011; Ottman, 2017)

2.7. Evaluation And Conclusion

This section demonstrates that digitalization is redefining brand strategies across operational, semantic, and ethical dimensions. A brand is no longer just an identity;**It is a living system that exists in the triangle of data, experience and community.**

While brand image was a controllable concept in the traditional period; It has become a collective construction process in the digital age. Consumers are not just buyers; He is the co-author of the brand's story. For this reason, brand strategy in the digital world should be built on the principles of sustainable trust, meaning production and ethical integrity.

As a result, strong brands in the digital age are those that can connect with humanity, not technology. Of course, we will also use technology to establish this connection. However, we should not forget that the being we call human is a being that has emotions, feels, is affected and affects. In this respect, we should use technology as a tool while determining brand strategies and managing the brand, as well as take into account the structure, perceptions, expectations, desires and feelings of people.

CHAPTER 3

DIGITAL BRAND MANAGEMENT AND BRAND BUILDING IN THE DIGITAL WORLD

1. INTRODUCTION

With the impact of digitalization, brands have had to reshape traditional management approaches and develop strategies suitable for the digital age. Digital brand management; It refers to an approach supported by technological infrastructures, based on multi-channel communication strategies and centered on customer experience.

Brand management in the digital environment does not only mean publishing the digital version of the logo or slogan. This process requires a consistent, reliable, and distinctive representation of the brand across all interaction points across digital platforms. All touchpoints such as the website, mobile application, social media accounts, digital advertising campaigns, and e-commerce infrastructure should be managed as a whole.

The omni-channel approach is at the heart of this process. The consumer is no longer only in physical stores with a brand; It also interacts through social media, mobile applications, chatbots, e-mail newsletters and digital advertisements. Therefore, the brand experience must be consistent, synchronized and delivered in high quality across every channel.

Digital brand management is also based on a data-driven structure. Targeted marketing strategies can be developed by analyzing consumer behavior, digital traces, interaction history, and feedback. This allows brands to offer personalized experiences to the consumer. Personalization is critical for brand loyalty and satisfaction.

Brand personality is also being redefined in the digital landscape. The tone, language, sense of humor, social responsibility approach and attitude of the brand in times of crisis become evident in digital communication and directly affect consumer perception. At this point, it is of great importance that social media managers act in harmony with the strategic identity of the brand.

The construction of brand image in digital environments is now directly related to content production. Content marketing plays a key role in conveying the brand's areas of expertise, values, and culture to the target audience. Blog posts, videos, infographics, social media content, and influencer collaborations are valuable in this context.

In addition, user-generated content (UGC) is one of the most powerful factors affecting brand image. Consumers sharing their experiences about the brand on social media directly affects the perception of new consumers and increases brand credibility. Whether a product is sold or not is not only related to its price, quality or meeting needs. The most important factor affecting sales performance is consumer confidence. Therefore, first of all, an audience should be created for the brand, then this audience should be prepared for the brand, then the image should be strengthened by building the brand and efforts should be made to make consumers trust the brand. If you pay attention, we have not mentioned the product that will be produced and put on the market. If this structure is designed first and then production and market presentation are carried out, it will be observed that the sales performance is much better.

When all these elements come together, digital brand management is a multi-layered process that should be carried out on the axis of strategic integrity, technical infrastructure, content production, data analytics and communication consistency. Successful digital brand management is not only visible; It is possible to provide a meaningful, consistent and sustainable brand experience.

2. CONCEPTUAL FOUNDATIONS OF DIGITAL BRAND MANAGEMENT

Digital brand management is an integrated management approach that goes beyond the boundaries of traditional brand strategies and redefines the brand on the axis of data, technology and human experience. Digitalization has not only transformed marketing tools, but also radically changed the meaning of the brand, its communication language, the way it produces value and the relationship it establishes with the consumer.

Aaker's (1991) **brand identity model** emphasizes that a brand is not just a name, logo or symbol; it is a holistic reflection of the organization's values, vision, culture and relations with the consumer. Today, this integrity is now managed through digital touchpoints. Brands are not limited to physical stores or traditional media campaigns; It creates a continuous flow of digital experiences through websites, mobile applications, social media platforms, email marketing, chatbots and interactive content.

In the past, brands used to plan one-way campaigns to reach consumers, but today, thanks to data analytics, algorithmic targeting, artificial intelligence-supported customer segmentation and real-time interaction tools, they instantly monitor and analyze the behavior of consumers and take strategic positions accordingly.

This transformation has transformed the brand from a static identity **into a dynamic, learning and evolving organism.**

The Customer-Based Brand Equity approach developed by Keller (2001) suggests that associations, perceptual network structure, and emotional experiences form the basis of brand equity. Digitalization has made this perceptual structure both more complex and more measurable. Brands now use new metrics (engagement rate, sentiment analysis, brand advocacy index, etc.) that measure brand value through social media interactions, user-generated content (UGC), online comments, influencer shares, and digital community behavior.

As Kapferer (2012) states in his "brand pyramid" approach, brands exist not only through product performance or advertising language, but also through the way they create meaning. The digital age has transformed this production of meaning into a multi-layered process. Now, brands have gone beyond being storytellers and have become active producers of digital culture. Netflix's content strategies, Apple's user experience design, or Nike's digital community practices (such as Nike Run Club) show that brands are turning into cultural identity generators.

2.1. Three Basic Axes of Digital Brand Management

The concept of digital brand management is generally structured on three strategic axes in the literature. These axes are technological infrastructure, data and insight management, and experience and communication integrity approaches.

1.   Technological Infrastructure

The technological infrastructure that makes up the digital ecosystem of the brand is the basic ground of strategic branding. Website architecture, customer relationship management (CRM) systems, e-commerce platforms, social media management tools, data analytics panels, and artificial intelligence-based decision support systems are the basic components of this infrastructure. Thanks to these systems, the brand traces every digital contact it establishes with the consumer and produces behavior-based insights. This infrastructure is not just an operational tool but a resource that nurtures the brand's strategic acumen.

2.   Data and Insights Management

At the heart of digital brand management is "information".**Big Data, artificial intelligence (AI)** and machine learning (ML)-based analytics show brands not only what happened in the past, but also what may happen in the future. In this way, brands can develop proactive strategies by anticipating consumer trends. As Hollebeek and Chen (2014) emphasize, digital interaction is not only a form of information sharing, but also a form of emotional investment. Brands should combine analytical intelligence with emotional connection strategies to create data-based but human-centered decision mechanisms.

3. Experience and Communication Integrity

Digitalization makes the brand not only visible, but alsoIt has transformed it into an experiential being. User interfaces, mobile app designs, voice assistant integrations, social media language, visual identity, and content formats directly reflect the brand's personality. Coherence and emotional alignment are the foundation of this experience integrity. The value a brand promises on its website should not clash with its social media tone, customer service response language, and physical store atmosphere. In the digital age, "brand personality" can only build trust through this integrity.

Table 4. "A Meaning-Producing, Data-Driven and Human-Focused Digital Brand Ecosystem"

A Meaning-Producing, Data-Driven, and Human-Focused
Digital Brand Ecosystem

The diagram below summarizes the "Conceptual Framework of Digital Brand Management". In the first circle, the components of "Data and Insight Management (Information), in the second circle, "Technological Infrastructure (System) and in the third circle, "Human Experience and Interaction (Meaning)" are shown. The intersection of these three areas represents the center of digital brand management: **The main qualities at the intersection, which can be defined as** the "Meaning-Producing, Data-Supported and Human-Touching Brand Ecosystem":

- Strategic vision and value proposition
- Technological competence and analytical intelligence
- Emotional attachment and trust-based communication
- Brand identity that is constantly learning and adapting

2.2. Brand Interaction in the Digital Age: Co-Creation

Digitalization has transformed brand management from a one-way narrative to a process of mutual production. Hollebeek and Chen (2014) state that digital brand interaction is not just a marketing tool, but a "co-creation space" where the consumer makes an emotional investment in the brand. Now, instead of passively listening to brands' stories, consumers are rewriting and sharing them. This process strengthens the sense of belonging to the brand and turns the consumer into a "participant" of the brand. For example, the LEGO Ideas platform allows users to contribute to the brand's product development process by presenting their own designs. Similarly, Starbucks shapes its product innovations directly through its customers' suggestions through digital feedback applications.

2.3. Strategic Outcome and Institutional Scope

Digital brand management has become not just a marketing activity but a holistic component of corporate strategy for today's businesses. Digitalization is a transformative force that directly impacts the organizational structure, decision-making processes, and corporate culture of the brand. This transformation has led brands away from traditional hierarchical structures and towards more agile, **data-driven and human-centered organizational models.**

Today, brand value is shaped not only by external marketing performance, but also by factors such as internal digital maturity, information management capacity and employee experience. Thus, digital brand management serves as a strategic bridge that balances the brand's internal culture and external perception. The experience offered by the brand to the consumer is a reflection of the extent to which the organization is integrated into digitalization in its internal processes.

In this context, digital brand management is positioned at the intersection of three basic components:

1. Strategic Vision

Brand positioning, value proposition, and identity alignment are all part of a multidimensional strategic vision in the digital age. Brands now have to position not only their products but also their digital experiences. The value proposition is not limited to functional benefit but also encompasses the meaning that the brand represents in the digital environment. Therefore, the brand vision should explain not only "what it offers", but "why it exists" and "what kind of value world it represents". For example, Tesla's vision of sustainable energy or Apple's mission to empower creativity directly align with the brand's digital communication strategies. Such **integrity positions the brand's strategic orientation not only in the market but also in social consciousness.**

2. Technological Proficiency

The sustainability of digital brand management is directly proportional to the brand's adaptation power to technology. Data infrastructure, digital analytical tools, and agile system integration form the foundation of the brand's competitive advantage. Big Data, AI-powered forecasting systems, customer relationship management (CRM) software, and digital dashboards enable brands to measure consumer behavior in real-time and produce personalized experiences. This technological prowess not only enhances operational efficiency; It also makes strategic decision processes data-based. Therefore, digital brand management requires making technology an integral part of the brand's strategic identity rather than investing in technology.

3. Anthropocentrism

People are at the center of all digitalization processes. Digital brand management sees the consumer not only as a target audience but also as an active stakeholder participating in the brand's meaning production process. Building emotional connections, enriching the user experience, and building sustainable loyalty are fundamental to the brand's long-term success. In this context, user experience (UX), user interface (UI) design, personalized communication, and digital community management have become tools for human-centered brand management. Additionally, the digital competence of in-house human resources directly impacts brand identity. How employees represent the brand's values in the digital environment is one of the factors that determine the consistency of the brand in the outside world.

These three components—strategic vision, technological proficiency, and human-centeredness—form the intersection of digital brand management. This space represents not only "existing" in the digital world, but also producing meaning and building trust. In this sense, digital brand management redefines the corporate identity paradigm of the 21st century. Brands have now become organisms that are **"culturally digitalized, technologically agile, touched by people in terms of communication, and strategically driven by data"**.

As a result, digital brand management is no longer just a marketing approach; it has become an organizational philosophy that covers all functions of the organization and is shaped on the axis of culture, ethics and technology. Brands are obliged to manage not only to "exist" in the digital environment, but also to create a meaningful, reliable and human impact. This transformation has brought with it the paradigm of "creating meaning with data", which constitutes the essence of modern branding.

4. OMNI-CHANNEL APPROACH AND EXPERIENTIAL CONSISTENCY

The omni-channel approach refers to brands creating **an "integrated, synchronized, and seamless customer experience"** between physical and digital touchpoints. Technological transformation and digitalization have transformed consumer behavior from linear to a multifaceted, cyclical, and simultaneous structure. Now, a consumer does not interact with the brand only on one channel; It is in a constant transition between website, social media, mobile app, physical store and e-commerce platforms. In this context, omni-channel requires the brand **to offer "one voice, one identity, and one experience"** across all these channels (Verhoef, Kannan & Inman, 2015).

In the traditional "multi-channel" model, each channel is managed independently, while in the omni-channel model, all touchpoints are part of an integrated strategic system. For example, a consumer can add a product they see on Instagram to their cart on the mobile app and pick it up in a physical store. The uninterrupted progress of this process depends on the perfect functioning of the brand's technological infrastructure (CRM integration, stock management, data synchronization).

Lemon and Verhoef (2016) define omni-channel experience as "an integrated value chain that ensures consistency at every stage of the customer journey". This chain; It covers all stages of awareness, consideration, purchase, experience and loyalty. Therefore, the omni-channel approach is not only the integration of sales points, but also the management of the continuity of the relationship established with the consumer.

The success of an omni-channel brand strategy is shaped in three main dimensions:

1. **Data Integration and Insight Management:** Each channel collects different data from the consumer. Integrating this data in a unified database allows the brand to achieve a "single customer view". Thus, brands can recognize the consumer on every platform and convey consistent messages.

2. **Experiential Consistency and Brand Identity: In** the digital age, brand identity is not just measured by the logo but by the emotional values reflected in every aspect of the user experience. The website's design language, store atmosphere, social media tone, and customer service tone should create the same emotional impression. This requires the brand to act in "sensory and perceptual harmony".

3. **Real-Time Synchronization and Flexibility:** The digital ecosystem has a dynamic structure; therefore, omni-channel structures should be managed flexibly based on instant data flow. For example, a stock change or campaign update should be reflected simultaneously on all platforms. This is critical for both operational excellence and reliability.

Omni-channel strategies create not only technical integration but also emotional continuity. If the experience with a brand in the store contradicts the perception in the digital environment, cognitive dissonance occurs in the consumer's mind. Therefore, consistency is not only a visual or textual phenomenon, but **also an experiential and emotional phenomenon.**

In this context, many global brands have set an example with their omni-channel practices:

Starbucks integrates loyalty programs in physical stores with its mobile app, offering a personalized experience across both digital and physical channels.

Sephora creates "personal beauty profiles" by matching users' online shopping history with the in-store experience.

Apple constructs its digital store, Genius Bar and Apple Store designs with the same minimal aesthetic and experiential integrity approach.

These examples show that the omni-channel approach means not only "multi-channel sales", but also telling the brand story with the same emotional depth at every point. The ultimate goal of omni-channel brand management is to provide the consumer with **an uninterrupted** meaning and value experience, not just a product or service. In this context, the powerful brands of the digital age are not those that multiply their touchpoints; It is the brands that connect these points.

CHAPTER 4

DATA-DRIVEN BRAND MANAGEMENT AND PERSONALIZATION STRATEGIES

Digitalization has transformed brand management from intuitive decision-making processes into a data-driven, measurable, and predictable structure. Today, brands create strategies by analyzing not only historical sales data but also consumer digital behaviors, search trends, social media interactions, and emotional reactions. This new structure transforms the brand from a "talking institution" to a **"learning organism"** (Wedel & Kannan, 2016).

4.1. Big Data and Strategic Decision Making

Data-based brand management is fundamentally based on the concept of "big data". Big data refers to the huge sets of information obtained from consumers' digital footprints (clickstream), social media activities, mobile application usage and online purchasing behavior. This data is used in brand strategies for four main purposes:

1. **Consumer Segmentation:** Demographic-based classical segmentation has been replaced by behavioral and psychographic analysis. With the help of algorithms,

brands identify consumers with similar behavior patterns as micro-segments.

2. **Predictive Analytics:** Artificial intelligence and machine learning models offer brands the opportunity to develop "preventive" strategies by predicting consumer future behaviors.

3. **Campaign Optimization: With** real-time data, campaign performances are instantly measured and dynamically adapted.

4. **Loyalty Programs and Value Optimization:** Data analytics calculates Customer Lifetime Value (CLV), ensuring the most efficient allocation of resources.

Wedel and Kannan (2016) defined this process as "the transformation of data into strategic intelligence" and emphasized that brands are no longer managed only by marketing departments but **also by data science teams.**

4.2. Personalization and Experiential Marketing

One of the most powerful components of digital branding is the personalization strategy. Personalization is the customization of a brand's communication, content, and offerings at an individual level based on the consumer's behavioral history, preferences, and contextual data. This approach establishes a one-to-one experiential relationship between the brand and the consumer (Kotler, Kartajaya & Setiawan, 2017). Personalization occurs on three levels:

1. **Content Level:** User-specific messages, product recommendations, or dynamic page designs are presented on websites and social media.
2. **Product Level:** Amazon's "Those who bought this product also bought" algorithm or Spotify's "Discover Weekly" lists are examples of this practice.
3. **Service Level:** Personal contact is provided in customer service through chatbots, CRM-based reminders, and digital assistants.

Data-driven personalization doesn't just drive sales growth;**It builds emotional connection and trust. Loyalty is strengthened when the consumer feels that the brand "gets" them. According to Lemon and Verhoef (2016), this is the "empathetic" stage of the digital customer experience.**

4.3. Data Ethics, Transparency and Trust Element

Data-driven management comes with significant ethical responsibilities. Transparency about the collection, processing, and use of consumer data is one of the most critical trust criteria of the digital age. Keller and Swaminathan (2020) emphasize that brand trust cannot be sustained without "ethical data governance." Here are the key principles that brands must adhere to:

1. **Consent: The** use of personal data without explicit consent from the consumer is unethical.
2. **Transparency:** The purpose for which the data is collected should be clearly stated.
3. **Data Security:** Cybersecurity measures are a key factor in protecting brand reputation.

Facebook's Cambridge Analytica scandal is a concrete example of how violating data ethics can cause significant reputational damage to brands. For this reason, modern brands should act with a sense of ethical responsibility, not just legal ones, in their data collection processes.

4.4. Example Apps: Netflix, Amazon, and Nike

Netflix analyzes user viewing history and preference behavior to provide personalized movie recommendations. This system has increased user satisfaction by over 80% and placed the "recommendation algorithm" at the center of brand identity.

Amazon personalizes the experience based on user behavior with dynamic pricing and product recommendation systems, which uses machine learning algorithms.

Nike enhances user engagement with personal goals, achievement badges, and feedback through its mobile app, Nike Run Club. This strategy is a digital loyalty model that reinforces the brand's theme of "individual motivation".

These examples show that personalization is not just a sales strategy, but an emotional component in the construction of brand identity.

4.5. Strategic Importance of Data-Driven Brand Management

Data is a new "form of capital" for brands in the digital age. This capital is not only a statistical resource, but also a mechanism for generating strategic insights. Through data analytics, brands anticipate consumer needs, personalize communication, optimize operations, and create a competitive advantage. However, the most powerful output of data-based brand management is **"relationship depth"**. Brands that know the consumer's history, understand their preferences and predict their behavior sell not only products but also meaningful experiences. In conclusion, when data-driven brand management and personalization strategies are combined, brands are not just digitalizing, **they** are achieving human-centric digital intelligence.

CHAPTER 5

BRAND PERSONALITY AND COMMUNICATION LANGUAGE IN DIGITAL ENVIRONMENT

Brand personality is a symbolic identity formed by attributing human qualities such as people to a brand. Aaker (1997) defines brand personality as "the sum of human characteristics that consumers visualize in their minds when perceiving the brand". These characteristics are generally classified into five main dimensions. These;**sincerity, excitement, competence, sophistication** and ruggedness. In traditional marketing, brand personality is mostly shaped by advertising language, visual identity and product experience, while in the digital age, this personality lives and transforms through direct interaction.

5.1. Redefining Brand Personality with Digitalization

The digital environment has made brands not only visible but also **interactive entities. In this new order, brand personality is no longer a one-way message;**it is an identity that is constantly reproduced with the consumer.Kapferer (2012) describes a brand as a "living organism", which expresses itself in the digital world through content production, social media dialogues, campaigns and crisis management. Social media platforms are the areas where brands showcase their personalities most openly.

- Twitter/X represents the humorous, reactive and quick-thinking aspect of brands;
- Instagram, its **aesthetic, emotional and story-based aspect;**
- LinkedIn is **corporate, professional and trust-oriented;**
- TikTok **offers an opportunity to represent its innovative, young and fun side.**

In this context, brands must create an upper tone that aligns with their overall brand identity while showcasing a distinct "micro-personality" on each digital platform. Consistency is the most fundamental characteristic of a digital brand personality.

5.2. Digital Communication Language and Tone Management

Brand communication of the digital age is not only verbal;**It has turned into an emotional, symbolic and contextual form of communication. A brand's language on social media, the words it uses, emojis, its visual style, and even its responsiveness reflect its personality.**

Brand language consists of three layers:

1. **Discourse Level (Verbal):** The words used, the form of the messages and the intonation.

2. **Visual Level:** Color, typography, photographic style and symbolic expression.

3. **Behavioral Level:** The way the brand responds to the user, its approach to the crisis and its capacity to empathize.

Holt (2016) says that modern brands are obliged not only to produce messages, but also to create cultural participation. Therefore, digital brand language is as much about **"how it behaves"** as it is about **"what it says"**. For example, while Wendy's brand uses sarcastic, humorous language on Twitter to connect with the younger audience through humor, Apple maintains the dimension of **"sophistication"** with a simple, formal, and aesthetic tone. Netflix is strong in the dimension of **"sincerity"** with its use of community-based, heartfelt language enriched with cultural references.

5.3. Digital Brand Personality in Times of Crisis

Crisis management is the area where digital brand personality is tested most prominently. A brand's attitude towards mistakes, criticisms, or negative comments provides strong indicators of the brand's character. The emotional intelligence of a brand in the eyes of the consumer is measured by the tone of language in the moment of crisis. Brands that empathize, admit their mistakes, and approach solution-oriented gain trust, while brands that deny or take an aggressive stance lose their digital reputation.

Schultz and Block (2015) define digital crisis management as **"the reflection of brand personality under stress"**. Therefore, the brand's crisis strategy should be consistent with the brand identity and maintain the triangle of **"sincerity – transparency – solution"** in communication.

5.4. Humor, Empathy, and Social Sensitivity

In the digital age, the communication language of brands is not only about providing information but also about creating emotional resonance. Humor, empathy, and social sensitivity have become essential components for the language of modern digital brands. Humor gives the brand a humanizing characteristic. Empathy enables emotional intimacy. Social sensitivity creates moral legitimacy.

For example, **Nike**'s Colin Kaepernick campaign "Believe in something. Even if it means sacrificing everything." It has reinforced the brand's brave, determined and justice-oriented personality with social sensitivity. Similarly, Ben & Jerry's has clarified its ethical-political identity in the digital environment by taking an active stance on social justice and environmental issues. However, for such campaigns to be effective, there must be consistency between the actions of the brand and its statements; otherwise, the perception of "ethical insincerity" occurs (Parguel, Benoît-Moreau & Larceneux, 2011).

5.5. Design Principles of Digital Brand Personality

Digital brand personality is created through strategic design, not random language selection. This process is based on five key principles:

1. **Consistency:** Brand language should reflect the same values across all digital channels.
2. **Adaptability: While** the tone may vary across different platforms (e.g., LinkedIn – professional, TikTok – fun), the main identity should be maintained.
3. **Empathy:** Language that the consumer can establish an emotional connection with strengthens the "human" face of the brand.
4. **Authenticity:** Imitation or stereotyped language undermines digital trust.
5. **Cultural Adaptation:** The language should resonate with the local culture; it should observe universal values.

These principles make the brand's digital presence not only recognizable but also felt. As Kapferer (2012) points out, brand identity in the digital age is not just a "visual representation" but a behavioral consistency.

5.6. Conclusion: Digital Persona, Digital Reputation

Digital brand personality is one of the determining elements of the long-term reputation of modern brands. The language a brand uses online, the reactions it gives, the values it embraces and the attitude it takes on social issues constitute its "character file".

Consumers no longer perceive brands as institutions, **but** as digital entities that behave like people. For this reason, brands with a strong digital personality, consistent language and empathy accumulate emotional capital. This capital is brand trust and reputation value, which is much more enduring than short-term sales .

CHAPTER 6

CONTENT MARKETING AND DIGITAL BRAND BUILDING

Content marketing has become not just a component of brand building in the digital age, but a backbone element. Pulizzi (2012) defines content marketing as "the planned production of valuable and consistent content in order to attract a specific target audience and establish long-term relationships with them". This definition summarizes the direction of modern branding: brands no longer sell products, they **sell knowledge, meaning and experience.**

6.1. Conceptual Basis of Content Marketing

Traditional marketing depends on what the brand says; Digital marketing, on the other hand, focuses on what the brand is telling. This difference sets content marketing apart from classic advertising. Advertising creates short-term awareness, while content marketing builds long-term trust and authority (Holliman & Rowley, 2014).

In Keller's (2001) "Customer-Based Brand Equity" model, brand equity is associated with the associations formed in the consumer's mind and perceived expertise. Content marketing is a strategic tool that feeds this network of associations. A brand gains cognitive trust through content that generates knowledge, guides, and benefits its community.

Kapferer (2012) defines a brand as "an identity system that produces meaning". In this context, content marketing makes the brand's identity sustainable with the integrity of the stories it tells. In other words, content becomes the reason for the existence of the brand, not the "tone of voice".

6.2. Content Types and Strategic Objectives

Content marketing in digital brand building is multi-layered and consists of formats that serve different purposes. This diversity enables brands to carry out not only promotion but also relationship management and meaning production processes. Holliman and Rowley (2014) state that content strategy has a three-functional structure: "informing, persuading and inspiring". A successful digital brand balances these three functions in content planning.The basic types of content can be classified as follows:

Table 5. Content Types, Purposes, Sample Applications

Content Type	Purpose	Sample Applications
Educational Content	Information sharing, perception of expertise	HubSpot blogs, Google Primer
Story Telling	Emotional connection, conveying brand values	Patagonia "Don't Buy This Jacket" campaign
Visual Content (Video, Infographic)	Engagement and viral spread	Red Bull Extreme Sports videos
Community Engagement Content	User engagement, UGC promotion	LEGO Ideas platform
Influencer Collaborations	Trust transfer, new audience reach	Nike x Travis Scott collaboration

6.3.   Brand Storytelling and Emotional Connection

The most powerful aspect of content marketing is that it makes the brand a "storyteller". Brands embody their intangible values through the story; establishes an emotional bond with the consumer. In this process, content not only conveys information but also **creates a sense of identity and belonging.**

Holt (2004) argues that brands build identity through cultural stories in his "cultural branding" theory. In this context, the examples are quite striking:

- **With the theme of** "transcending human limits", Red Bull has reinforced the image of adrenaline and freedom with content.

- **Patagonia** tells the value of sustainability through story-centered documentary content.

- **Coca-Cola** transforms the concepts of sharing and happiness into emotional stories with the theme of "Open Happiness".

In the digital age, these stories are reproduced with user contribution through social media; In other words, the brand starts the story, and the community continues it. This has ushered in the era of "participatory narrative" in digital brand building.

6.4.   Influencer Marketing and Trust Transfer

One of the most effective extensions of content marketing is influencer collaborations. While consumers trust advertising messages less and less, they attribute higher credibility to the content of digital opinion leaders. This phenomenon indicates that trust is now moving from institutional authority to individual authority (Freberg et al., 2011).

Influencer marketing is not just promotion; it is the representation of brand values through social identities. If brands resonate with the language, attitude, and community culture of the influencer they choose, this relationship strengthens the brand personality. However, making the wrong choice can create perceptual conflict in brand identity. Therefore, the influencer strategy should be designed as carefully as the brand identity.

6.5.   Authenticity and Trust in Content Marketing

The modern consumer seeks authentic (real and sincere) **content, not just aesthetic or interesting**." "Real stories", "user experiences" and "behind-the-scenes posts" strengthen the sincerity of the brand. This approach makes the brand human and accessible rather than flawless.

Keller and Swaminathan (2020) describe the impact of authenticity on digital brand image as "emotional trust building." The brand should present a statement of value, not just information, with its content. This is decisive for the brand's long-term reputation and loyalty.

6.6. Measurement and Optimization of Content Marketing

The success of content marketing is measured by data. Brands evaluate content performance with metrics such as click-through rate (CTR), engagement rate, conversion rate, and content sharing level. These metrics allow the brand to understand which types of content have a stronger emotional connection. Tools like Google Analytics, HubSpot, Sprout Social, and Hootsuite are essential systems used in content performance management.

Data-driven content strategy continuously evolves with the cycle of "experiment – analysis – adaptation". Pulizzi (2012) summarizes the success of content marketing as "strategic storytelling sustained with consistency".

6.7. The Role of Content in Digital Brand Building

Content marketing is the most powerful strategic tool of digital brand building. Brand, through content; it tells its own story, delivers value to its audience, builds community, establishes trust, and ultimately builds a lasting digital identity. Strong brands no longer only produce products, they act as media institutions that produce meaning. Red Bull Media House, HubSpot Academy or LEGO Ideas are pioneering examples of this transformation. These brands have been able to multiply their brand value by placing content production at the center of their corporate strategies. Content is not just a communication tool for a digital brand, it is the narrative of its raison d'être, and when this narrative is built on consistency, authenticity and meaning, the brand image becomes permanent.

6.8. User-Generated Content (UGC) and Digital Trust

User-Generated Content (UGC) is one of the phenomena that radically changes the understanding of brand communication in the digital age. UGC means that consumers share their experiences, opinions or creative productions about the brand in the digital environment. These contents are; It covers a wide range from social media posts to blog posts, from product reviews to YouTube videos.

Christodoulides (2009) defines UGC as "the new form of brand management in which brand meaning is now produced jointly not only by businesses, but also by consumer communities". This approach has transformed digital branding from a one-way communication to a participatory culture.

6.9. Participatory Culture and Consumer Authority

Digitalization has shifted the power of producing information and content from brands to consumers. Consumers are no longer just buyers, but also content creators, critics, and brand ambassadors. This phenomenon is defined as "participatory culture" (Jenkins, 2006).

While the brand image was built from top to bottom by the business in classical times, this process is shaped within a horizontal sharing network in the digital age. The brand now becomes the collective creation of its community. For this reason, modern brand managers have to carry out not only "message control" but also community management and meaning governance.

The most important effect of UGC is that it strengthens the authentic (real and reliable) perception of the brand. Because people trust the experiences of other users rather than the brand's own advertising. According to Nielsen's 2023 Global Trust in Advertising report, 92% of consumers find user reviews more trustworthy than brand ads

6.10. The Role of UGC on Brand Trust

Digital trust is one of the key factors that determine a brand's reputation. Keller and Swaminathan (2020) define brand trust as "the consumer's belief that the brand will deliver the value it promises." UGC is directly instrumental in building this trust; Because these contents do not pass through corporate filters and reflect the real user experience. The contribution of UGC to brand trust can be examined at three levels:

1. **Cognitive Trust:** The consumer makes a rational assessment about the quality of the product or service through the comments of other users. For example, having thousands of user reviews about a hotel reduces the consumer's perception of risk.

2. **Affective Trust:** Real user stories create sincere feelings towards the brand. When a user turns their positive experience with the brand into a video, this content creates emotional intimacy in other consumers.

3. **Community Trust:** UGC strengthens the interaction of digital communities formed around the brand. These communities constitute the brand's "social proof" mechanism (Cialdini, 2009).

CHAPTER 7

SOCIAL PROOF AND PERCEPTUAL LEGITIMACY

Social proof is the tendency of people to accept a phenomenon as "true or reliable based on the behavior of others." In the context of branding, this means that user content creates "perceptual legitimacy". For example, when thousands of people produce positive content about a product, it creates a collective approval effect on the brand.

Reviews indicate that over 70% of consumer purchasing decisions in the digital landscape are driven by UGC (Bazaarvoice, 2022). In this context, UGC is no longer just a promotional tool; it has become a strategic trust-building mechanism.

7.1. Brand-Community Interaction and Shared Value Creation

UGC is not just a "feedback" tool for brands; it is a **co-creation** platform. Consumers can develop new ideas, product designs, or campaigns by collaborating with the brand. Some successful examples of this process include:

- **Starbucks – "My Starbucks Idea" Platform:** More than 300 innovations have been implemented with the suggestions of the users.
- **LEGO – "LEGO Ideas":** User designs are submitted to the voting system; winning projects are released to the market.
- **GoPro:** It has created a "consumer-generated brand identity" by building all brand communication on user videos.

These examples demonstrate that the brand can create a participatory brand culture by sharing its authority. Muniz and O'Guinn (2001) define such communities as "brand communities" and emphasize that these communities reproduce the brand's identity.

7.2. UGC Management and Strategic Risks

While UGC can strengthen the brand, it can also pose reputational risks if mismanaged. Negative reviews, inaccurate content, or misinformation can damage a brand's digital trust. Therefore, brands should manage their UGC strategy according to these principles:

1. **Transparency:** User content should not be filtered but should be moderated within ethical boundaries.

2. **Ethical Use:** Users' content rights should be respected (Creative Commons and copyrights).

3. **Incentivization for Participation:** Positive UGC generation should be supported by reward, engagement, or sharing mechanisms.

Successful brands consider user content not only as "impressions" but also as a means of common meaning production.

7.3. The New Source of Digital Trust: Community Authenticity

The modern consumer believes in people, not advertisements. UGC redefines this trust:

Corporate brand trust turns into →community-based trust.

Brand image →becomes the sum of user perception.

Loyalty →It is built on the experience of co-production and sharing.

This transformation has made brands no longer only communicating but also **listening and co-producing with actors. UGC transforms the brand into a "telling" entity, not a "telling" one.**

7.4. Conclusion: Trust and Loyalty in a Participatory Brand Ecosystem

User-generated content is the strongest indicator of brand trust and reputable communication in the digital age. For brands, trust is no longer just a matter of quality or promises; it is an in-community verification process.UGC is at the heart of this process. Therefore, digital brand management should see UGC not only as a marketing tool, but also as a digital democracy mechanism. Because trust is no longer the common property of the brand, but the common property of the community.

CHAPTER 8

TRUST, CONSISTENCY, AND MEANING IN DIGITAL BRAND BUILDING

In the digital age, brand value is built not only on visibility or interaction, but also **on the triangle of trust, consistency,** and meaning. These three concepts are the pillars of the "reputation architecture" that makes the brand's digital presence sustainable. Keller and Swaminathan (2020) define brand trust as "the consumer's belief that the brand will deliver the value it promises." This trust has become more fragile in digital environments because every interaction of the brand is now public, traceable, and interpretable. A misstep can turn into a global perception crisis in seconds. That's why digital trust is **built with data, behavior, and consistency, not just words.**

8.1. Dimensions of Digital Trust

Digital trust has a multi-layered structure and can be examined at three basic levels:

1. **Corporate Trust:** It is based on the brand acting legally, ethically, and transparently. Data privacy, respect for consumer rights, and ethical marketing practices are key indicators of this level.

2. **Interactional Trust: It** is associated with sincerity, empathy, and honesty in communication with the consumer. The tone of dialogues conducted on social media, statements during a crisis, or the approach of customer service are the visible face of this trust.

3. **Perceptual Trust:** It is related to how "consistently" the consumer perceives the brand in their mind. When there is a mismatch between brand promises and experience, trust is damaged. Iglesias and Ind (2016) define this situation as a "crisis of perceptual incoherence".

8.2. Consistency: The Silent Power of Digital Branding

Consistency is the internal harmony that the digital brand establishes between "discourse, visual identity, and behavior". This concept strengthens the brand's digital identity on both semantic and experiential levels. Kapferer (2012) defines consistency as "the connective tissue that maintains brand identity." Consistency, beyond visual elements such as logo, color palette, typography, also encompasses the continuity between the brand's value statement, ethical attitude, and communication language.

Inconsistent brands lose trust in the digital environment because consumers now want to see the same message on every channel: Brands that use a different tone on their website, a different tone on social media, and a completely different tone in their crisis statement experience "identity disintegration". This leads to a weakening of digital trust and a loss of brand credibility. Therefore, consistency is the invisible but most powerful stability mechanism of digital brand identity.

8.3. Meaning and Value-Based Branding

Modern brands are no longer just economic players offering products or services; they **have become cultural organisms that produce value. Iglesias, Ind, and Alfaro (2013)** define meaningful branding as "the process that associates the brand purpose with social and individual values".

A brand's ability to create meaning in the digital world is based on three basic axes:

1. **Purpose:** Associating the reason for the existence of the brand not only with profit but also with social benefit and ethical values. For example**, Patagonia** has transformed environmental awareness into its brand identity with the motto "we do business to save the world".

2. **Value Alignment:** The brand's stance on social issues should coincide with the target audience's values. Conscious consumers of the digital age perceive even the silence of brands as an "attitude".

3. **Authenticity:** The harmony between the brand's statements and actions determines the credibility of the meaning. Superficial approaches such as greenwashing and socialwashing are the most rapidly noticed reputation mistakes of the digital age (Parguel et al., 2011).

Meaning-based brands create an existential connection, not an emotional one. The consumer not only prefers such brands; identifies with them.

8.4. The Interplay of Trust, Consistency, and Meaning

These three concepts have a cyclical structure that reinforces each other:

- **Consistency** is the foundation of trust.
- **Trust** ensures the sustainability of meaning.
- **Meaning** increases the emotional commitment capacity of the brand.

Sirdeshmukh, Singh, and Sabol (2002) emphasize that trust is not based solely on past experiences but on **expected consistency. In other words, the consumer trusts the brand not because it will "always remain the same", but because he "believes that he will act consistently in every situation".**

This perspective brings with it the necessity of brands to "be human" in the digital age. Brands that are sincere, accountable, take responsibility when they make mistakes, and do not remain silent on social issues gain trust.

8.5. The New Paradigm of Digital Reputation: Meaningful Trust

The maturity level of digital branding is no longer measured by brand awareness, but **by the level of meaningful trust**. This concept means that the brand is not only reliable, but also **meaningfully reliable. In other words, trust is an emotional bond; meaning points to the moral basis of this bond.**
Brands that build meaningful trust:

- Manages their data ethically,
- He harmonizes his actions with his words,
- It takes a sincere stance in the fields of social responsibility and sustainability.

Such brands gain long-term legitimacy not only with consumers but also within digital communities and the media ecosystem. Therefore, digital trust is no longer a communication strategy; **it's the moral fabric of brand identity.**

8.6. Conclusion: Digital Trust, New Brand Capital

In the digital world, trust is the most valuable "invisible asset" of the brand. Consistency ensures the sustainability of this trust; meaning gives it depth. When these three elements come together, the brand becomes not only a preferred but also a respected asset.

In Kapferer's (2012) words, "brands are no longer obliged to tell who they are, but to prove who they are." Therefore, the ultimate goal of brand management in the digital age is to **build a sustainable reputation based on meaningful trust.**

CHAPTER 9

DEPARTMENT EVALUATION AND CONCLUSION

In this section, the transforming structure of digital brand management is discussed holistically, from its conceptual foundations to its implementation strategies. The global digitalization process is not only the way brands communicate; It has radically changed the methods of building identity, personality, value, and trust. Brands are no longer defined only by "what they sell", but by what kind of meaning they build.

Digital brand management represents a strategic paradigm shift. While traditional branding is based on planned message generation and one-way communication, the brand understanding of the digital age is based on the foundations of interaction, data analytics, community engagement, and experience management. This shift has transformed the brand from a passive institution to an active digital **organism. This organism is a structure that learns, listens, reacts, and develops.**

8.7. Conceptual Transformation: Understanding from Data

As discussed earlier in the chapter (3.1–3.3), digital brand management now requires data-driven strategic intelligence. Big data analytics, machine learning, and CRM systems make it possible for brands to recognize their consumers not only as a "target audience" but also as individuals with behavioral and emotional aspects. This process lays the foundation for personalized experiences, moving the brand from rational planning to intuitive empathy. Therefore, data has become not only a resource for modern brands but also strategic capital that builds relationships.

8.8. Experiential Integrity: Omni-Channel and Digital Identity

Omni-channel strategies create a seamless experience chain by integrating brands' physical and digital assets. The success of this chain depends on the brand maintaining the same emotional tone, aesthetics, and value integrity at every touchpoint. Consistency is the **silent guardian of** brand trust, not just corporate identity. **As emphasized in the section, the consumer no longer exists between channels, but** in the flow of experience; therefore, the brand has to maintain the same emotional echo in this flow.

8.9. Digital Personality and Meaning Production

Brand personality is no longer a static image, but an interactional character. Brands speak, react, make mistakes, and learn digitally just like humans. Therefore, digital communication language is the most powerful tool that reveals the "human side" of the brand. Elements of sincerity, humor, empathy, and social sensitivity make the brand an emotional "living identity" in the consumer's mind. In this context, meaning production redefines not only marketing performance but also the reason for the brand's existence.

8.10. Content and Community: An Era of Participatory Branding

Content marketing and user-generated content (UGC) are practical reflections of this transformation. Brands are no longer the sole narrator, but the coordinator of the collective story. The consumer becomes a part of the brand through content production and sharing. This strengthens not only the reliability of the brand but also its authenticity. UGC, as the most powerful "social proof" mechanism of the digital age, gives the brand both visibility and legitimacy. Therefore, modern branding is not a "communication process"; it is the management of a participatory culture.

8.11. Trust, Coherence, and Integrity of Meaning

The ultimate goal of digital branding is to build lasting trust. This trust is no longer just about quality or performance; **It is measured by ethical attitude, transparency, data privacy, and cultural responsibility. In Kapferer's (2012) words, brands are no longer obliged to "tell who they are, but to prove who they**

are". In this context, meaningful brands are not only preferred but defended. The consumer not only establishes an emotional bond with these brands; he also feels a sense of belonging to the values they represent.

8.12. A Perspective for the Future: The Age of Digital Emotions

As a general conclusion of the chapter, it can be said that digital branding is not only a technological transformation, but also **a transition to the age of emotional intelligence.** Artificial intelligence, big data, and automation tools provide information to brands, but lasting success will be for brands that can blend this knowledge with human sensitivity. Digital brands of the future; They are structures that empathize with data, produce meaning with content, share value with communities, and most importantly, build trust with ethics. For this reason, the measure of creating a strong brand in the digital world is no longer just "awareness", **but palpability. Felt brands last longer than visible brands. Because the trio of trust, loyalty, and meaning constitutes the new brand capital of the digital age.**

CONCLUSION

In an era where the digital world moves at relentless speed and perceptions are formed in seconds, brands are no longer defined solely by the products or services they offer. They have evolved into carriers of meaning, emotion, and narrative. Throughout this book, it has become clear that sustainable brand strength does not emerge from technology alone, but from a deep understanding of human behavior, values, and expectations. Digital tools may amplify a message, but they cannot create meaning by themselves. What ultimately gives a brand its value is not the sophistication of its algorithms, but its ability to resonate with people on an emotional level.

The digital age provides brands with unprecedented visibility, access, and data. Yet visibility should never be mistaken for significance. Real success lies not in being constantly seen, but in being genuinely remembered. Memorability is built through trust, consistency, authenticity, and purpose. These elements cannot be engineered overnight, nor can they be sustained through short-term tactics. Digital brand management, therefore, should be understood as a long-term strategic discipline focused on nurturing an invisible yet powerful bond between brands and individuals. This bond is formed where rational value propositions intersect with emotional relevance.

As explored throughout the chapters of this book, digital platforms are not merely communication channels but living environments where brands are continuously interpreted, judged, and redefined by their audiences. Every interaction, response, visual, and message contributes to the broader brand perception. In such an environment, coherence becomes critical. Brands that lack a clear identity or fluctuate in tone and values may achieve temporary attention, but they struggle to earn lasting loyalty. In contrast, brands that articulate a clear purpose and express it consistently across digital touchpoints are better positioned to build credibility and emotional attachment.

The journey of digital brand building is neither linear nor easy. Competition is intense, consumer expectations evolve rapidly, and technological change is constant. Trends rise and fade, platforms lose relevance, and algorithms are repeatedly reconfigured. However, amid this volatility, one truth remains stable: emotions endure longer than technologies. People may forget a campaign, a slogan, or a platform, but they rarely forget how a brand made them feel. Brands that manage to embed themselves into personal experiences, values, and memories gain a form of resilience that technology alone cannot provide.

Ultimately, brands that carry a sense of soul, purpose, and human understanding are the ones that move further and last longer. They do not chase attention aggressively, but earn it patiently. They do not speak louder than others, but speak more meaningfully. In the digital world, where noise is abundant and attention is scarce, depth becomes a competitive advantage. Meaning becomes strategy.

And perhaps the most important reminder for the future of brand management is this: brands do not exist merely to leave a mark on the world, but to create space in the hearts and minds of people. When a brand achieves that, it transcends platforms, survives technological shifts, and becomes truly timeless.

And let's not forget: **"Brands exist not to leave a mark on the world, but to make room in the heart of the person."**

REFERENCES

Aaker, D. A. (1991).*Managing brand equity: Capitalizing on the value of a brand name.*New York: Free Press.

Aaker, J. L. (1997). Dimensions of brand personality.*Journal of Marketing Research, 34*(3), 347–356.

Bazaarvoice. (2022).*Shopper experience index.*Bazaarvoice Research Report.

Brakus, J. J., Schmitt, B. H., & Zarantonello, L. (2009). Brand experience: What is it? How is it measured? Does it affect loyalty?*Journal of Marketing, 73*(3), 52–68.

Christodoulides, G. (2009). Branding in the post-internet era.*Marketing Theory, 9*(1), 141–144.

Cialdini, R. B. (2009).*Influence: Science and practice*(5th ed.). Boston: Pearson.

Fournier, S. (1998). Consumers and their brands: Developing relationship theory in consumer research.*Journal of Consumer Research, 24*(4), 343–373.

Freberg, K., Graham, K., McGaughey, K., & Freberg, L. A. (2011). Who are the social media influencers? A study of public perceptions of personality.*Public Relations Review, 37*(1), 90–92.

Hollebeek, L. D., & Chen, T. (2014). Consumer brand engagement in social media: Conceptualization, scale development and validation.*Journal of Product & Brand Management, 23*(7), 497–505.

Holliman, G., & Rowley, J. (2014). Business to business digital content marketing: Marketers' perceptions of best practice.*Journal of Research in Interactive Marketing, 8*(4), 269–293.

Holt, D. (2004).*How brands become icons: The principles of cultural branding.*Boston: Harvard Business School Press.

Holt, D. (2016). Branding in the age of social media.*Harvard Business Review, 94*(3), 40–50.

Iglesias, O., & Ind, N. (2016). How to be a brand with a conscience: Building a meaningful brand through authenticity and consistency.*Journal of Brand Management, 23*(4), 384–398.

Iglesias, O., & Ind, N. (2016). Towards a theory of conscious brand co-creation.*Journal of Brand Management, 23*(6), 488-506.

Iglesias, O., Ind, N., & Alfaro, M. (2013). The organic view of the brand: A brand value co-creation model.*Journal of Brand Management, 20*(8), 670–688.

Jenkins, H. (2006).*Convergence culture: Where old and new media collide.*New York: NYU Press.

Kapferer, J.-N. (2012).*The new strategic brand management*(5th ed.). London: Kogan Page.

Keller, K. L. (1993). Conceptualizing, measuring, and managing customer-based brand equity.*Journal of Marketing, 57*(1), 1-22.

Keller, K. L. (2001). Building customer-based brand equity.*Marketing Science Institute.*

Keller, K. L., & Swaminathan, V. (2020).*Strategic brand management: Building, measuring, and managing brand equity*(5th ed.). Pearson.

Kotler, P., Kartajaya, H., & Setiawan, I. (2017).*Marketing 4.0: Moving from traditional to digital.*Hoboken, NJ: Wiley.

Labrecque, L. I., Esche, J., Mathwick, C., Novak, T. P., & Hofacker, C. F. (2013). Consumer power: Evolution in the digital age.*Journal of Interactive Marketing, 27*(4), 257-269.

Lemon, K. N., & Verhoef, P. C. (2016). Understanding customer experience throughout the customer journey.*Journal of Marketing, 80*(6), 69–96.

Leonidou, C. N., & Hultman, M. (2011). Environmental marketing strategy and its relation to firm performance: An exploratory study.*Journal of Business Ethics, 104*(3), 283–297 - *Journal of Business Research, 64*(12), 1637-1643.

Mangram, M. E. (2012). The global auto industry and Tesla Motors.*Journal of Business Case Studies, 8*(1), 57-70.

Muniz, A. M., & O'Guinn, T. C. (2001). Brand community.*Journal of Consumer Research, 27*(4), 412–432.

Ottman, J. A. (2017).*The new rules of green marketing.*Sheffield: Greenleaf.Parguel, B., Benoît-**Moreau, F., & Larceneux, F. (2011).** How sustainability ratings affect brand equity.*Journal of*

Business Ethics, 102(1), 15-28.

Parguel, B., Benoît-Moreau, F., & Larceneux, F. (2011). How sustainability ratings affect brand equity: The case of environmental labelling.*Journal of Business Ethics, 102*(1), 15–28.

Pine, B. J., & Gilmore, J. H. (1999).*The experience economy: Work is theatre and every business a stage.*Boston: Harvard Business School Press.

Pulizzi, J. (2012). The rise of storytelling as the new marketing.*Publishing Research Quarterly, 28*(2), 116–123.

Schmitt, B. (1999). Experiential marketing.*Journal of Marketing Management, 15*(1–3), 53–67.

Schultz, D. E., & Block, M. P. (2015). Potential impact of brand interaction factors on brand equity in social media.*Journal of Brand Management, 22*(9), 755–772.

Sirdeshmukh, D., Singh, J., & Sabol, B. (2002). Consumer trust, value, and loyalty in relational exchanges.*Journal of Marketing, 66*(1), 15–37.

Verhoef, P. C., Kannan, P. K., & Inman, J. J. (2015). From multi-channel retailing to omni-channel retailing: Introduction to the special issue on multi-channel retailing.*Journal of Retailing, 91*(2), 174–181.

Wedel, M., & Kannan, P. K. (2016). Marketing analytics for data-rich environments.*Journal of Marketing, 80*(6), 97–121.*